"Buchalter offers a rich resource bursting with ideas for mandala making with clients. The simple, easy to use themes and media techniques for group and individual work are practical and varied. With sensitivity to the centering and insight achievable through mandala making she suggests directives that embrace the archetypal dynamics of art making in a circle. This book will be a dependable guide for art therapists and mental health professionals alike."

—*Joanna Clyde Findlay, Art Therapist and Psychotherapist in private practice, co-author of* Art Therapy Relational Neurobiology Studio Art Therapy Approaches *(2013)*

"This is one of the most comprehensive books I have read on the mandala as a therapeutic tool. As an art therapist who has used mandalas for many years, I was amazed by the vast number of new applications and ways of using mandalas that are presented throughout this book… I am tempted to try any number of these strikingly original ways of using the mandala in groups or with individuals in my practice. The author includes directions and instructions, pictures and in depth analysis of mandala artwork, each with a special focus. The mandala, no matter in what way it is used, has a special power and people are drawn to it. What is different about this book is the multitude of ideas and different projects and ways of using the mandala drawing that are offered, and are accessible to both the layman and the professional therapist."

—*Phyllis Frame, Art Therapist and Director of Round Oaks Creative Center, Charlottesville, Virginia*

by the same author

Art Therapy Techniques and Applications
Susan I. Buchalter
ISBN 978 1 84905 806 3
eISBN 978 1 84642 961 3

A Practical Art Therapy
Susan I. Buchalter
ISBN 978 1 84310 769 9
eISBN 978 1 84642 004 7

Art Therapy and Creative Coping Techniques for Older Adults
Susan I. Buchalter
ISBN 978 1 84905 830 8
eIBSN 978 0 85700 309 6

of related interest

Art Therapy in Asia
To the Bone or Wrapped in Silk
Edited by Debra Kalmanowitz, Jordan S. Potash and Siu Mei Chan
Forewords by Shaun McNiff and William Fan
ISBN 978 1 84905 210 8
eISBN 978 0 85700 449 9

Art Therapy Exercises
Inspirational and Practical Ideas to Stimulate the Imagination
Liesl Silverstone
Foreword by Brian Thorne
ISBN 978 1 84310 695 1
eISBN 978 1 84642 693 3

Art Therapy and Anger
Edited by Marian Liebmann
ISBN 978 1 84310 425 4
eISBN 987 1 84642 810 4

Spirituality and Art Therapy
Living the Connection
Edited by Mimi Farrelly-Hansen
Foreword by Deborah Bowman
ISBN 978 1 85302 952 3
eISBN 978 0 85700 449 9

Mandala Symbolism and Techniques

Innovative Approaches for Professionals

Susan I. Buchalter

Jessica Kingsley *Publishers*
London and Philadelphia

First published in 2013
by Jessica Kingsley Publishers
116 Pentonville Road
London N1 9JB, UK
and
400 Market Street, Suite 400
Philadelphia, PA 19106, USA

www.jkp.com

Library of Congress Cataloging in Publication Data
Buchalter, Susan I. (Susan Irene), 1955-
  Mandala symbolism and techniques : innovative approaches for professionals /
Susan I. Buchalter ;
introduction by Alexandra R. Katz.
      p. cm.
  Includes bibliographical references and index.
  ISBN 978-1-84905-889-6 (alk. paper)
  1. Art therapy. 2. Stress management. 3. Stress (Psychology) 4. Mandala. I. Title.
  RC489.A7B825 2013
  615.8'52--dc23
                                2012031172

British Library Cataloguing in Publication Data
A CIP catalogue record for this book is available from the British Library

ISBN 978 1 84905 889 6
eISBN 978 0 85700 593 9

Printed and bound in Great Britain

Contents

Preface

Mandala art and meditation have been practiced for thousands of years by many cultures and religions. It has proven to be healing and enlightening. The circle represents nature and life giving forces such as the sun and moon, the earth, the universe and the womb. The mandala represents the circle of life and wholeness. It reminds us of the impermanence of life and the need to accept change. The mandala provides a sense of calm and comfort, focus and insight.

Creating mandalas benefits clients in numerous ways; some of the advantages of such work include healing, gaining insight and integration of one's inner and outer worlds. Designing mandalas helps clients form psychological boundaries; they are better able to define their own space and separate from other people when needed. Mandala art provides clients the opportunity to stay in the moment instead of allowing their thoughts to wander. Creativity, decision making, and problem solving are enhanced. Drawing mandalas helps individuals organize their ideas and goals. Psychological growth is developed, and a sense of inner balance is restored. Clients are better able to express feelings, thoughts, hopes, fears, and dreams when they create mandalas; their stress level and anxiety decreases.

The meditation process becomes easier for many individuals because they have a personal object they can focus upon. The mandala is usually brightly colored and often eye catching. Mandala work helps support integration of one's inner and outer worlds. It aids in personal growth, transformation, and expansion of self-awareness. Self-esteem is increased as individuals honor their inimitable art and unique selves. Mandalas have proven to be revitalizing. Positive energy is used as participants choose which colors, shapes, and images to utilize in their work. The drawing, in and of itself, provides a vehicle to expend anxious energy while retaining healthy energy. Mandala work enables clients to focus on their inner thoughts instead of dwelling on external preoccupations.

Patterns of color, which may relate to thinking and feeling, are observed, and inner wisdom and spiritual growth are enhanced. Mandala work can lower blood pressure and reduce tension; it helps individuals overcome barriers so they do not stay stuck in the victim role. This type of art helps quiet the mind, and assists participants to express gratitude and love of life. Mandalas are enjoyable to design and they help people make connections within themselves and with others. Mandala art provides the structure that enables individuals to reflect on their life. Carl Jung believed that "Mandalas are an outward projection of the psyche, representing a safe refuge and movement towards psychological growth and healing" (Jung 1973).

Clients tend to feel more comfortable working within the circle because it is structured and defined. They frequently feel comfortable when boundaries are set. Individuals who may not ordinarily draw will be more willing to participate because they view the mandala as "doable." Mandalas help clients understand that their work, like themselves, is unique and accepted unconditionally in the art room. Many people feel freer to reveal true feelings when drawing a mandala, and less likely to hide behind superficial images such as vases of flowers and landscapes. They are often able to find artistic patterns, which reflect behavior and personality. This new knowledge and insight is used to facilitate self-awareness, leading to positive life style and attitude changes. When clients create mandalas they are able to utilize them as "mirrors to their souls."

The projects presented are diverse and useful for various populations. The therapist will assess which exercises are appropriate for their clients. Most of the exercises will take from 45 to 60 minutes. The timing depends on the clients' diagnoses, their abilities, and the therapist's time frame. Some directives may be completed in two or three sessions if need be. Under *Materials* I do not include a paper plate (the mandala template) because that will be standard for almost every project. The group leader may determine the size of the plate; I prefer a standard size.

As I have mentioned in my other publications, one should not view this collection simply as a "cookbook" of therapeutic techniques. Readers should take it as a challenge to add their own personal touches in order to create sessions that are most meaningful for their particular clientele and themselves. The more ideas the therapist has at his or her fingertips, the easier it will be to lead a successful therapeutic group. Therapists may modify, change, and combine ideas at their discretion. Group leaders will decide which mandala directives are too difficult; they will need to take into consideration the clients' abilities, attitude, and psychological state. The group format and exercises must adapt accordingly.

Therapists, psychologists, counselors, social workers, students, teachers, and holistic healers would benefit from reviewing this publication. The vignettes provide readers with descriptions of the mandalas and associated feelings. They help the reader understand the client's experiences, feelings, and points of view.

The chapters focus on different types of mandala interventions, such as stress reduction and collage work. I refer to group members interchangeably as clients and patients, although there are some therapists who do not care for these labels. I also refer to the therapist as "he" to avoid the more cumbersome "he/she." I do not mean to discriminate in any manner. It is important to refer to the reference section when indicated because some of the projects will need modifications that are suggested in this area. An example would be a project that might be considered helpful for someone diagnosed with clinical depression, but not for someone diagnosed with bipolar disorder. The information may not be included in the immediate project description due to the specified book format.

When reading through the mandala directives, it is essential to understand that they are designed for a wide range of clients. Some interventions may be geared toward higher functioning clients, while others are geared toward a lower functioning group. It is up to the therapist to decide what is best for their own clientele.

Acknowledgment

Special thanks to Dr. Alan H. Katz for his usual outstanding technical support.

Introduction

Mandala is a Sanskrit term that is believed to translate to "circle" in English. Used as an aid to meditation, mandalas are thought to originate in conjunction with ancient Indian beliefs concerning the importance of the center as a sacred space from which a cosmic power can enter a figure. Mandalas have historically been used by Hindus and Buddhists as aids for meditation, although the mandala has taken many forms throughout history. It is associated with many cultures and is a part of various religions, from ancient times to the present. For Buddhists, the circle is a reflection of the samsara, which is the eternal cycle of life that can only be escaped if one achieves enlightenment. The Tibetan word for mandala is Kyil-Khor, which translates to "center and surrounding," and is traditionally used by Buddhists during sadhana meditation. Sadhana meditation helps individuals reach various levels of spiritual realization, or enlightenment.

Since Buddhism rejects a reliance on material objects, Tibetan Buddhist monks will create intricate sand mandalas over which they meditate and then destroy, sweeping the sand into a body of water as a way to demonstrate the impermanence of all existence. In Tibetan this form of art is called *dul-tson-kyil-khor* and translates to "mandala of colored powders." Creating the sand mandala takes a great deal of work and concentration usually spanning a period of several days. The meditation over the mandala is meant to help one achieve a sense of inner peace and tranquility by helping to reject the egocentric view of the world and rather reflect on sunyata, or emptiness. Without accepting sunyata over the physical world, it is thought to be impossible to achieve enlightenment. The mandala is also a sacred symbol for Native Americans. For the shamans, the center of the circle, or hoop, holds sacred healing power. In Christianity and Islam, the circle is used in various divine symbols such as the Celtic cross, the halo, and the dome.

The circle is one of the most immediately recognizable shapes in the universe and was recognized by medieval scholars as a divine or perfect shape. It is the basis of so many structures in the universe, from atoms and cells through stars and galaxies. It promotes relaxation because there are no boundaries, it is the most symmetrical two dimensional shape in existence, and unlike squares or rectangles, the circle can be rotated in any direction and remains the same. The circle does not have distracting corners or complex points so it is easy to focus on the center.

According to Peter Patrick Barreda, any mandala consists of a density of particles surrounding a central point, called the bindu, which represents the observer as a single point in the universe. In this way, mandalas need not conform to any single stereotype of appearance. Each individual can become the center of their own universe, or mandala, and from there demonstrate through art the thoughts and feelings that act as the essential particles of that individual's personal universe. While Buddhist monks must follow very strict and detailed instructions concerning how mandalas must be constructed and which colors must be used in which circumstances, mandalas that are used for therapy have no limitations. There is no right or wrong way to create a personal mandala, just as no two people see the universe in quite the same way. The mandala helps each person reflect on his or her own thoughts and emotions without focusing on outside influences as they "shut out the outside and hold the inside together." Therefore, the mandala offers a platform for complete freedom and a lack of pressure to create an image uniform with any mainstream definition of art.

Carl Jung, the father of analytical psychology, found that mandalas can be products of the unconscious. They are irrational and almost magical in nature, and, in his book *Memories, Dreams and Reflections*, Jung described the mandala as "the exponent of all paths. It is the path to the center, of individuation" (Jung and Jaffe 1962). As a natural part of the universe, the mandala symbol is also a natural part of each person's psyche. Because of a consistent pattern of individuals turning to the mandala symbol without prompting all throughout the world from the beginning of history to the present, Jung explains that the mandala symbolism is likely a part of what he describes as the collective unconscious.

Acting as a manifestation of the unconscious, the mandala can be an extremely useful tool for demonstrating a visible representation of unconscious thoughts. Once visualized, these thoughts can then be confronted and analyzed on a conscious level. David Fontana in his book *Meditating with Mandalas* (2009) explains that a mandala can be an aid for meditation "only if you allow it to do so." As we grow up we are taught many ways to control our lives and the world around us, but the goal of using mandalas for meditation is to dissolve layers of mental barriers and allow us to find the source of our troubles that were hidden in our subconscious mind.

Carl Jung explained that the mandala forms in the mind as a natural mechanism to help heal disorder in the unconscious during traumatic times by helping individuals discover a centrality to which everything else is related. The order and balance found through the mandala creation process helps soothe patients experiencing chaotic psychological states. He further explains that mandalas often have a significant therapeutic effect on their authors, although he makes sure to point out that the mandalas must be made spontaneously rather than planned or imitated. Jung goes on to suggest that the symbols and motifs present in patient-created mandalas are unknown to the patient until they look back on what they have drawn and analyze the possible significance of the images they have drawn.

Mandalas may be drawn spontaneously and instinctively (such as traditional mandalas) or created with specific themes, but in a therapy situation directed themes can be powerful tools. Mandalas offer a paradoxical combination of structure and freedom.

Alexandra R. Katz, BA

Chapter 1

Drawing

Drawing mandalas allows the client the opportunity to communicate thoughts, feelings, concerns, problems, wishes, hopes, dreams, and desires in a relatively non-threatening manner. The mandala serves as a safe vehicle to express unconscious as well as conscious issues and beliefs. Creative expression through mandala art provides the individual with the freedom to represent his inner and outer world in any way he chooses. There are no judgments and the client is told that however he chooses to draw is perfectly acceptable. The individual is informed that he may use stick figures, line, color, shape, abstractions, or realism to portray his thoughts. A variety of materials such as markers, oil pastels, crayons, and 11″×14″ (28×36cm) drawing paper are presented. In this way clients can decide which materials to use. Decision making is very important; it helps enhance problem solving skills, and increases independence and self-esteem.

Taking time to discuss the artwork allows clients to observe, analyze, and relate to representations and figures illustrated. It provides for group interaction and feedback from others. Group members are able to reflect on the symbols drawn, and thoughts may be conveyed that would otherwise not be shared verbally. The mandalas serve as a compilation of feelings, problems, concerns, and solutions that are exclusively the client's own. Images serve as vehicles, which facilitates communication, growth, and insight.

Standard mandala

Materials: Drawing paper, crayons, pastels, and paper plates.

Procedure: Have clients trace a circle from a plate or draw their own circle free hand. Ask them to color in the circle starting in the center and working their way toward the periphery of the circle.

Discussion/goals: Goals include centering, focusing and expression of feelings through design, color, and images.

Figure 1

A male client in his 60s, named Mike, drew this very meticulously designed mandala. This client had been an engineer before he retired due to a variety of disabilities including barbiturate addiction. He used a semicircular ruler to create even lines and repeated the same pattern a number of times to create this design. During discussion he stated that he was a perfectionist and everything had to be "just right." He erased the lines a number of times before he was "semi-satisfied" with his design. He also insisted on showing the group leader how to create the mandala using his method.

Mike stated that he enjoyed creating this mandala. He shared that he liked the sharp spikes because they appeared strong and menacing. Mike stated that when he was growing up he had to be tough because his neighborhood was filled with "kids who were bullies. You had to at least pretend to be powerful or they would eat you up alive. I learned to put on a mean face and be ready to pounce before I was 12 years old. I did carry a knife, but it was only a small pocketknife. Still, I felt it gave me a feeling of safety and self-assurance." Mike remarked that the mandala seemed powerful. The circular containment was helpful in that Mike needed structure in order to feel safe. He said that the spikes (anger) could "go on forever." When asked what he saw in the mandala, Mike remarked that he saw an explosion and related the explosion to his anger. He was angry with himself for becoming addicted. He viewed himself as weak because of his addiction and disabilities, which included arthritis and memory problems. He said that when he was working he was "looked up to," "but now, no one sees me; I am just a speck of dust in the wind." When asked to analyze the mandala further, Mike was able to observe certain positives such as a center that seemed to be in control of the rest of the artwork. He was able to relate the mandala center to his own core, and began to realize that it was his responsibility to gain control of his life and of "his spikes." Mike seemed a little more open to exploring anger management techniques and coping skills. He was asked to find some of his old strengths and utilize them now, but in a healthier manner, and in a style conducive to his present life style.

Positive and negative

Materials: Drawing paper, markers, crayons, and oil pastels.

Procedure: Group members fill in half of the mandala with positive colors and shapes, and the other half with negative colors and shapes.

Discussion: Have clients discuss the feelings that arise from viewing the opposite sides. Explore which side is most outstanding, which side was drawn first, and which side is most identifiable.

Figure 2

Jimmy, a 62-year-old man challenged with schizoaffective disorder, drew himself "happy and sad." The happy side of his face has a slightly upturned mouth, a heart on his cheek, red hair, and a small yellow sun containing a tiny red heart. The sun is connected to the side of his head. The sad part of his face contains a black shape on his cheek ("a scar") and a down turned mouth. His hair is purely black. Jimmy remarked that he's joyful when he has company, especially when he sees his brother and attends program. He mentioned that he doesn't own a television set, his radio works poorly, and he is almost always alone; he doesn't have friends. He even eats all of his meals alone in the local hospital cafeteria for a small fee. Jimmy shared that he often sits in the lobby of the hospital after dinner; sometimes he sits there until visiting hours are over. "At least this way I have something to do; I watch the people." Jimmy often stares at people as if he's in a trance. This may be represented by the piercing eyes he drew; they seem to be staring straight ahead. Jimmy doesn't understand subtle cues and has difficulty relating to others, yet he wants to be around people. When asked, he shared that the heart and sun represent the love he has for his brother and his hope to have a girlfriend one day.

Emotions I

Materials: Drawing paper, paper plate, markers, crayons, pastels, and pencils.

Procedure: Clients are asked to fill in the mandala with colors and shapes that represent various emotions they are experiencing or have experienced in the past.

Discussion/goals: Goals include healing, focusing, stress reduction, and sharing of emotions. Boundaries and appropriate expression of feelings may be explored.

Figure 3

Phil, a man in his late 60s diagnosed with clinical depression and suffering from some memory loss due to electroconvulsive therapy treatments, drew this colorful mandala he titled "Snowflake." Phil described the mandala as floating in space. He was able to relate to that theme because he didn't understand why he needed to be in the program and attending therapy groups. He mentioned he felt like he was "misplaced." He described the center of the mandala as the focal point. "This is where the movement is." He stated the "branches are expanding and growing outwards." When asked, Phil related this growth to changes in his life, some of which he was not pleased with at all. He was moving to a small apartment from a large house, and this change was quite difficult for him and his wife of 38 years. He stated they put so much effort into taking care of the house and adding additions; it was heartbreaking to sell it. Phil felt like his home was an extension of himself: "it was safe and comfortable." The lines surrounding the branches symbolized his need for organization and direction. He stated he was a perfectionist. His memory problems were very frustrating because in the past he was known for his superb memory. The green shapes surrounding the lines represented the feelings of calmness he was trying to attain, but having little success at doing. Phil stated he was very nervous and had difficulty sleeping. His appetite had decreased and his wife was worried about his weight loss. The oval shape behind the branches is colored yellow to represent "hope." The pink oval surrounding it represented Phil's love for his wife. He remarked that the lines drawn are pink, green, brown, and blue. "My moods vary, but mostly they are blue nowadays." He was asked by a group member to focus more on the lighter colors so he could think more positively. When asked about the empty space behind the amorphous shape he remarked that, that is the unknown. "I don't know what to put there. We'll see..."

Figure 4

Fred, a very charming man in his 30s, diagnosed with bipolar disorder, designed a self-portrait to portray emotions. He related the colors to various feelings. The yellow eyes symbolized "feeling better" and the blue checks represented "feeling more balanced." Fred was very pleased that his medication was helping him maintain control and better focus. He was slowing down at work; previously he had been working on many difficult projects at one time. In the past, Fred had been getting two to three hours of sleep each night and not taking time for family, relaxation, exercise, or proper meals.

There is an orange, smiling mouth that represents "happiness" and the turquoise semicircular lines near the cheeks are his "dimples." His hair, which is thinning, is orange and green, and his front part is composed of red lines. Fred included a brown goatee. He seemed proud of his goatee, saying it took him a long time to grow it perfectly. When another group member wondered about the dark blue cheeks, Fred remarked that the cheeks also represent dark days, which are diminishing. It is noteworthy that the cheeks are quite outstanding.

Fred was pleased with this portrait and felt it looked like him. He was able to acknowledge that he will have to be careful in the future; he will need to balance his life style in order to stay calm and in control. It is very easy for him to lose his focus.

Figure 5

This wild mandala was created by a bipolar client experiencing the manic phase of his illness. He greatly enjoyed this creative experience and shared his artwork proudly with group members.

Connecting dots

Materials: Drawing paper, black markers, colored markers, crayons, colored pencils, and oil pastels.

Procedure: Ask clients to use black marker to make a series of at least six dots about the size of a thumbnail within the mandala. They may be scattered or placed in a specific pattern. Then have clients connect the dots with straight or curvy lines. They may fill in the background with color if desired.

Discussion: Examine what type of design emerges from the connections. Explore how connecting the dots leads to problem solving and abstract thinking. Examine how people use "connecting the dots" to solve problems.

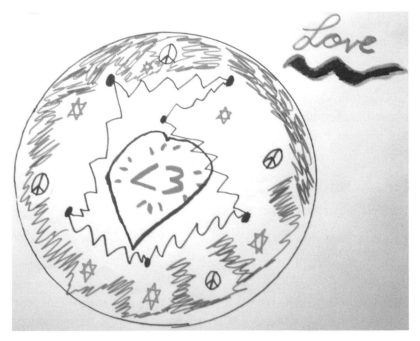

Figure 6

A male in his early 30s named Austin represented his recent break-up with his girlfriend of two years. The center heart, which is cracked, symbolizes the sadness he had been experiencing regarding this loss. He stated his heart actually hurts and feels heavy. "It is presently broken, but I think that it will heal in the future." The black squiggly lines surrounding the heart, connected by six black dots, represent Austin's ambiguous feelings toward his ex-girlfriend. He remarked that he feels both anger and sadness. He wants to call her and beg her to come back but he knows that would unhealthy and unwise. She made it clear that their relationship was over. She had met someone else and was actively dating him already. Austin stated he felt like finding the new boyfriend and "punching him in the nose." The black dots represent "the punches." The peace signs and Jewish stars in the background are what "helps me from hurting the new boyfriend or myself." Austin shared a love of religion and peace. He stated he is a very spiritual person who believes in karma and faith.

The green scribbled lines that compose the background represent Austin's "peaceful self." While viewing the mandala he expressed hope that he would find a new girlfriend in the near future whom he could trust and perhaps marry one day. He shared insights such as needing to be calmer, a better listener, and more open minded in future relationships. Although Austin titled the mandala "Love" the word "Love" is underlined in an angry-looking black and orange lightning bolt type of line. Designing the mandala helped him explore his feelings and responses to this situation. He was able to sort through a variety of emotions in a non-threatening manner.

Heart/mind

Materials: Drawing paper, markers, oil pastels, and crayons.

Procedure: Divide the circle in half. Have clients fill in one half of the circle with *what is in their heart* and the other half with *what is in their mind.*

Discussion: Explore similarities and differences between the heart and mind symbolism. Ask participants, "If the heart side of the mandala represents feelings and the mind side of the mandala represents thoughts, which one is stronger? Which one seems more important at the moment?" Observe how active or inactive the mind appears. Examine statements such as *feelings are not necessarily facts,* and *thoughts may positively or negatively affect our behaviors.*

Active mind/images

Materials: Drawing paper, markers, oil pastels, and crayons.

Procedure: Support participants to fill in the mandala with images and thoughts that are uppermost in their mind.

Discussion: Explore healthy and unhealthy patterns of thinking. Support clients to share memories and recurring thoughts and beliefs. Examine ways to stop "thought overload."

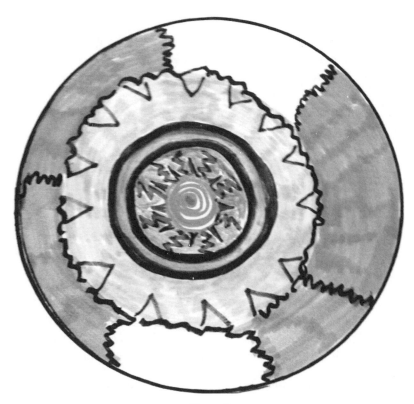

Figure 7
Mandala illustrated in the color insert

Marie, a 45-year-old woman who was dealing with a severe depression, drew a mandala symbolizing a series of thoughts about her road to wellness. The center of the circle is composed of a "rose spiral" representing Marie's "good nature." The squiggly red lines emanating from the center symbolize the angry thoughts Marie frequently experiences. Marie expressed much anger at family members for not understanding or supporting her throughout her depression. She stated that her niece and nephew, as well as her cousins, tell her to get a job and "snap out if it." They tell her she's lazy and a procrastinator. This greatly irritates and frustrates Marie, who feels misunderstood and rejected. The blue circle surrounding the pink flower and red squiggly lines represent a "safe place." Marie remarked that she protects herself from the criticism and negativity by isolating and blocking out her relatives' disparaging remarks.

The outer colors of the circle symbolize the way Marie would like to feel. As per Marie, the yellow is "happiness," the green is "peace," and the orange is "feeling alive." The triangular outlines within the orange circle represent obstacles to recovery. When asked, Marie mentioned that her sensitivity to what others think, her vulnerability and dependence on family members for approval, stand in her way of recovery. She titled her work "Trying to Get Out."

Anxious mind

Materials: Drawing paper, markers, oil pastels, and crayons.

Procedure: Have participants create a design "representing your mind when it is filled with anxiety." Encourage clients to think about patterns, lines, shapes, and colors.

Discussion: Observe how the anxious mind looks. Discuss how the shapes, patterns, images, and flow of the individual designs reflect stress. Explore what thoughts, feelings, and behaviors are associated with anxiety, and examine various ways to calm the mind.

An overweight woman in her early 50s named Anna, diagnosed with schizophrenia, designed this expressive mandala. Anna included a small sad face surrounded by a colorful starburst, which was surrounded by chaotic lines and scribbles. Anna was not able to identify realistically with the face, which she said was "happy." In actuality it appears sad, with a crooked mouth and eyebrows that rise and appear distressed. It almost looks trapped within the starburst and scribbles surrounding it. Ann remarked, when prompted, that the starburst surrounding the face is beautiful and reminds her of the stars in the sky. She went on to speak about previous vacations in the country. She shared that she would stare up at the stars at night and notice how large and striking they appeared. The scribbles reminded her of "a mess." Anna mentioned that sometimes she becomes very nervous and needs to take extra medication to calm her nerves. Sleep had been a problem for her until recently. She had been experiencing nightmares and early morning wakening. Once she woke up, she could not fall back to sleep, even if it was as early as 3:00am.

Figure 8

Anna shared that lately she had been sleeping better and feeling less anxious. She stated she used to feel ugly and she didn't have any friends, but since she met a new friend named Betty her mood has changed. She remarked that she has lunch with Betty and "Betty is good to her." Anna stated she feels better about herself because Betty likes her. She declared that Betty doesn't care how she speaks or what she looks like. She was able to title the mandala (with help from group members) 'Things are Better Now."

Figure 9

A 29-year-old woman named Terri designed this mandala to represent her anxiety and fear about the future. She symbolized herself as the tiny turquoise dot in the middle of the mandala. Terri remarked that the dot (herself) is small and insignificant. It looks overwhelmed by the designs surrounding it. She continued to share that she feels overwhelmed by her work situation as well as her family situation. She is a newlywed whose husband travels a lot. She didn't realize how much she'd miss him when he was gone and how lonely she would feel. Terri shared that she is beginning to feel "pangs of jealousy." She remarked that she is feeling envious of her husband's travels and wonders whether he is being faithful on his business trips. These thoughts are becoming more frequent, and are contributing to physical and psychological symptoms such as poor sleep, panic attacks, and over-eating. Terri mentioned that she has gained six pounds this past month because of the "junk food and snacks she eats in the evenings to self soothe." The lines surrounding the turquoise dot are shaky and quivering. When asked, Terri stated they symbolize her anxiety and her "low self-esteem." The outer rim of the circle is composed of green, yellow, and blue wavy lines. These lines are smoother and not as shaky. Terri remarked that she felt calmer when she began the last part of the mandala. The lines reminded her of waves gently breaking on the beach. Terri felt most anxious designing the middle of the mandala; it was difficult for her to draw and maintain a pattern. During group discussion Terri was able to acknowledge that she tends to be a perfectionist, which causes stress. She also acknowledged that she might benefit by not *assuming* her husband is being unfaithful. She stated she would gently confront him if she continues to experience concerns. Terri also acknowledged that she has strengths and needs to develop her self-esteem by focusing on herself, her capabilities, her friendships, and her work. Everything she attempts to do does not have to be perfect.

Stress release

Materials: Watercolor paper, watercolors, markers, and oil pastels.

Procedure: Create an image depicting a release of stress and anxiety.

Discussion: Examine the colors, size, and shapes represented. "Explore the strength of the anxiety and the impact it has on your life."

Moon mandala

Materials: A copy of a photo of the moon filling in most of an 8½"×11" (22×28cm) sheet of paper, markers, crayons, and oil pastels.

Procedure: Direct participants to fill in the photo of the moon in any way they please. Suggest they might design "The man on the moon," or what they think the moon would look like if they were actually there. They may create their unique version of what another planet may look like, an ideal world, or they may just use the outline to draw an abstract image or design.

Discussion: Explore how group members feel about our planet in terms of the environment, health, safety, and nature. Explore thoughts about the earth's relationship with the moon and other planets in the solar system. Examine the manner in which participants illustrated the moon and what it says about their quest to find a safe and secure place to live, their satisfaction with life on our planet, and goals and concerns for life in the future.

Mandala of abundance

Materials: Drawing paper, markers, oil pastels, and crayons.

Procedure: Have clients fill in the mandala with figures, images, and symbols of people, thoughts, gifts, treasures, and other items they cherish. Remind group members that intangible things like health and love may be included.

Discussion: Encourage participants to discuss the positive aspects of their life and the riches they possess. Explore values, desires, and needs. Ask the following question as the clients are analyzing their mandalas: "What is really important in life?"

A 40-year-old client named William, who had been dealing with a severe depression, stated he's thankful for his home, health, and his church. He remarked that he attends church every Sunday and is an active participant. The congregation accepts him unconditionally. This is crucial for William because his own family is not supportive and lives far away. He rarely sees his brothers, who berate him when he does visit with them. There is constant family conflict because they feel William should lead a more traditional life. They want him to get a full time job, stop feeling sorry for himself and find a wife. William stated he wants to be left alone; he's satisfied with his life as it is. He becomes frustrated because his family doesn't understand the nature of his disability.

William included his love of nature in his mandala by adding trees growing upward, unusual flowers, grass, bushes, the sun, a lake, and fish. He spoke about fishing on warm summer afternoons, and enjoying the peace and serenity of this activity. William remarked that he leads a simple, but pleasant life. It is noteworthy that the sun has two eyes and a nose but no mouth, and the house has two windows and a side door, but no front door. This may symbolize William's inability to reach out to others at the moment; he still has some work to do before his depression lifts and he's ready to fully participate in life and "let people in."

Figure 10

Pain

Materials: Drawing paper, markers, oil pastels, and crayons.

Procedure: Participants fill in the circle with symbols and images that represent physical and/or psychological pain. Ask clients to contemplate what pain might look like to them (colors, images, shapes, etc.).

Discussion: Explore each participant's artistic and verbal interpretation of pain. Examine internal and external factors that cause pain and methods to lessen and/or alleviate it.

Figure 11

A client named Toni represented her psychological turmoil. She stated she's very confused and "in limbo." Toni had just been laid off from her job as an administrative assistant in an accounting firm; she had worked there for eight years. She expressed concern because it was such a shock and her skills weren't up to date. The computer made her nervous; she only knew the absolute basics. Toni had little desire to learn anything new. She liked things "the way they were." Her teenage children were "driving her crazy." She stated they were "cutting school" and smoking marijuana. She felt she had no control over them. Every time she attempted to speak with them they became defiant. Toni characterized her husband as "fat and lazy." She was considering a trial separation. Toni remarked that all he did was work and lay on the couch. "That was his routine every day, nothing else." She was upset that at age 49 she didn't "know her life direction" and felt helpless. She stated she lost all her strength long ago.

The middle of the mandala represents her "thinking, the thoughts that go round and round in my head; they go nowhere." The bright colors surrounding the thoughts represent the people in her life who help her "stay together." "They keep the chaos from flooding out." Toni remarked that although her immediate family is a mess she has supportive friends, parents, and two supportive sisters. Her parents are represented by the yellow ovals, her sisters are the orange shapes, and her friends are the blue and green ovals. When she studied the mandala she said that it made her dizzy, that it was too busy. She did like the way the oval shapes held in the scribbles. When asked, she stated the border surrounding the chaos made her feel more secure.

Family

Materials: Drawing paper, markers, crayons, and oil pastels.

Procedure: Participants fill in the circle with family members and then add a background.

Discussion: Clients share which members were included, which were omitted, and the significance of the figures and background illustrated.

Hope and faith

Materials: Drawing paper, markers, oil pastels, and markers.

Procedure: Group members represent what hope and faith means to them through the use of symbols, shapes, words, and images.

Discussion: Explore the importance of having hope and thinking in a positive manner. Examine the power of the images depicted and each individual's associations to the images.

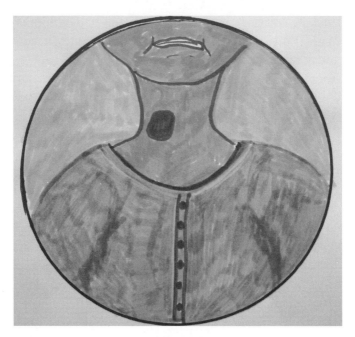

Figure 12

A 50-year-old, extremely anxious woman, named Felicia, focused on hope for her health. She recently woke up to find a lump on her neck. At first she thought it would go away, but after two weeks she decided it was time to visit the doctor who promptly sent her for an ultrasound. The ultrasound showed a complex cystic mass on her neck, but it was difficult to detect whether or not it was cancerous. The next step was to have a biopsy, which would occur in one week. Felicia seemed to think she had about a 60–40 chance ("60% cancer, 40% benign"). She was very fearful and more negative than positive, but stated she was hopeful the mass would be benign. "I pray every night it will not be cancer."

Felicia's mandala focuses on the mass on her throat. It is depicted as a large red ball. The rest of her body is lightly drawn in so all the emphasis on the lump. Felicia stated that although much of the focus is on the mass, the background of the picture is bright and cheery. The sun represented her wish that she will be okay, and the flowers represented "trying to have a positive attitude" and her desire for good health. She stated she has much to do in her life and wants to continue to grow and live. "I want to see grandchildren some day."

The flowers remind her of the positive people and "good things" in her life, and the knowledge that no matter what happens she has loved ones around her. She stated that she is really not as optimistic as the background of the picture, but she is trying her best. She stated she is trying to take one day at a time. When a negative feeling or thought pops into her head she tries to "shoo it away." When asked to title the work she called it "Praying for Health."

Nature mandalas

Materials: Drawing paper, markers, oil pastels, and crayons.

Procedure: Have clients fill in the mandala with drawn items such as flowers, trees, birds, plants, the sun and the moon.

Discussion: Explore themes such as growth, change, the environment, taking pleasure in everyday life and simple pleasures.

Figure 13

Esther, a 75-year-old woman who was overcoming a debilitating depression, represented her own recent growth in this mandala. Esther reflected on the artwork, stating she felt like she was beginning to live again and starting to enjoy her life. She remarked that for a long time she wasn't deriving pleasure from food, friends, or family, nothing made her smile or feel fulfilled. She had stopped volunteering and participating in senior clubs. She complained that she wasn't even able to taste her food; it all seemed very unappealing. She lost ten pounds (4.5kg) in less than a month. She kept to herself, sitting and staring at pointless television shows all day long. She didn't care about her appearance or even her hygiene. In the process of healing from her depression she slowly began feeling alive again.

When asked about the significance of the flowers, she mentioned that the four flowers in the mandala might represent her children, whom she adores, but has been unable to enjoy for the past three months. She shared that her two boys and two girls are her pride and joy. "They are amazing people." She related the stems and leaves to her grandchildren whom she hadn't seen for weeks because she didn't want them to see her so depressed. She stated that she was embarrassed by what she had become, "My appearance is horrifying." Esther was pleased with the movement of the mandala, especially with the flowers growing upward. She remarked that she hoped to improve both her mood and outlook, and to continue feeling better. During group discussion Esther stated she liked drawing within the circle because it felt safe. She remarked that she wasn't an artist but drawing within the circle helped her know where to begin and where to end the picture.

Forgiveness

Materials: Drawing paper, plate, markers, crayons, and oil pastels.

Procedure: Participants fill in the circle with images of what forgiveness looks and feels like to them.

Discussion: Support participants to discuss symbols in their art that reflects their attitudes toward forgiveness, and ask them to share times they have excused others for their wrongdoings. Explore how forgiveness may lessen anxiety and promote feelings of peace and a sense of well being.

Figure 14
Mandala illustrated in the color insert

A client in her early 60s named Lana drew a picture of her mother, age 86. Lana stated that her mother had always been self-centered, "I always came in second, and now it is still the same." Lana remarked that when she was young her mother worked even though her family was financially secure. She stated her mother always had an excuse to leave the house, whether it was work, a meeting, or going to the movies with a friend. Lana shared that she had to stay home and watch her younger brothers, even when she was as young as nine years old. "All the responsibility was placed on me." Lana remarked she remembered how her mother would dress up and take much time fussing with her hair and make-up, "It was very annoying to watch her." "I was not allowed to play with my friends so many times because I was the babysitter." Lana remarked that even though her mother is in her 80s she is still the same way. She is still narcissistic about her appearance and has had three plastic surgeries. "She looks good, but phony."

Lana looked at her mandala and sneered, "My mother really looks like that. She wears a lot of eyeliner and lipstick, lots of gold jewelry. Her cheeks are rouged and her eyebrows are way too high. Sometimes she looks a little spooky. She wears lots of jewelry and has a perm."

When asked what she would like to say to her mother, using the mandala as a mother symbol, Lana cried out, "You are selfish and I am angry at you. You never show me affection. You only care about yourself." After saying this Lana began to laugh because she thought her mother appeared so silly. She told group members that she was thankful she didn't look like her mother and she didn't have her personality. She stated she swore she would be a good mother and she felt she accomplished that goal. Lana also mentioned that her father wasn't home much either, but when he was home he was warm, funny and loving.

Fantasy

Materials: Drawing paper, markers, oil pastels, and crayons.

Procedure: Group members fill in the circle with representations of daydreams that include hopes, wishes, and desires.

Discussion: Clients explore their fantasies and examine how they reflect feeling, mood, behavior, and personality. Explore whether the fantasies may be achievable or unattainable. Examine how long individuals have had their fantasies and how they help or hinder their journey to get well. Discuss if clients have noticed a change in their daydreams in recent years.

Figure 15
Mandala illustrated in the color insert

Kami, a 61-year-old woman challenged with depression and probable borderline personality disorder, expressed her fantasy in this expressive and colorful mandala. Kami described the mandala as exuding high energy. The sun is expansive and showering its rays on most of the figures in the picture. Kami stated she wished she could feel enthusiastic and possess a lust for life. She yearned to have something to look forward to and the energy to see things through. She was hoping the sun's rays would help her grow and flourish, much like the tree, flower, and birds in the mandala. Kami remarked she wanted a man in her life and a family. She wished she could find someone to enjoy the outdoors with, and to have fun with on a daily basis. She complained that she was tired of being alone. She included a boat in her mandala to emphasize her desire to travel and enjoy nature. The tiny brown figure towards the right of the mandala is Kami. She stated she is just beginning to walk down the road that might take lead to her goal, but she has a long way to go before she achieves it.

Figure 16
Mandala illustrated in the color insert

Wilfred, a 65-year-old man challenged with bipolar disorder, designed his fantasy. He smiled and stated he'd like to live in a world with dinosaurs. He thought it would be amazing to walk out of his house and observe a tyrannosaurus, stegosaurus, or an apatosaurus. Wilfred remarked that if the dinosaurs were colorful it would be "even more fun." He filled the apatosaurus in with pink, orange, and green interweaving lines. Wilfred mentioned that as a child he studied dinosaurs and knew every name as well as what they ate and how they lived. He was known as "the expert," a title that he was most proud of having when he was in elementary school. Wilfred decided to create a "serene world" where humans and dinosaurs cohabitated happily together. He made sure to add green, blue, and pink trees, as well as large brown spiders that fly. When asked about the spiders, Wilfred remarked that they would not bite; they would be friendly and help the environment. It is significant to note that Wilfred would probably feel important in this imaginary world, especially being the dinosaur expert. He was recently retired and felt very insignificant and not sure what to do with his spare time. In his world he felt worthless.

Maori mandala

Materials: Drawing paper, oil pastels, markers, and crayons.

Procedure: Share with participants a little about the Maori tribe. After briefly discussing the Maori culture ask participants to design a Maori mandala, using spirals to convey their feelings and thoughts about the circle of life.

Discussion: Explore the personal messages conveyed through the spirals. Examine the clients' attitudes toward life, growth, and change.

Sun and wind

Materials: Drawing paper, markers, oil pastels, and crayons.

Procedure: Direct clients to draw a mandala that includes symbols of the sun and wind as the main part of the design.

Discussion: Explore the significance and power of the sun and wind, and how they are represented in the artwork. Examine the life giving energy of the sun and the free spirit and life force of the wind. Suggest clients discuss ways in which they can relate to the strength of these natural forces.

Yin yang[1]

Materials: Drawing paper, markers, oil pastels, and crayons.

Procedure: Clients fill in the mandala with both the male and female aspects of their personality.

Discussion: Group members explore the similarities and differences between their male and female side. Examine the effect the two sides have on identity, self-esteem, feelings, and behavior.

Figure 17

Katherine, an attractive woman in her 20s, focused on the anxiety and depression she was experiencing instead of representing the male and female aspects of her personality. She liked to do things her way and had difficulty following directions and listening to others. She was often abrupt, caustic, and appeared rigid. This rigidity was pronounced in her artwork, as she used a ruler to make sure the lines were as straight and equidistant as possible. Katherine stated the blue lines (the right side of the mandala) represented the depression she was experiencing and the pink horizontal lines (left side) represented "better days." Katherine remarked that she drew the pink lines in a horizontal manner to emphasize the difference in how she felt "then and now." "I used to be fun and outgoing, and now I don't feel or do anything." When asked, she remarked the circles filled in with dark green color represented her depression and dark moments. She stated she didn't like the way the circles looked. She felt they broke up the mandala; she remarked, "I wanted the lines to be continuous; this really bothers me." Katherine included the circles because "that's the way you have to make a mandala." This type of thinking represented her stiffness and inflexibility. Further therapy would focus on her rigidity and need for exactness and excellence in all her endeavors.

The web

Materials: Drawing paper, markers, crayons, and pastels.

Procedure: Instruct clients to draw a web (like a spider web) and place someone or something in it.

Discussion: Discussion focuses on who or what was placed in the web, how it feels to be stuck, and ways in which the client feels trapped. Goals include identification of problems, self-defeating attitudes, and exploration of coping mechanisms.

Candice, a 29-year-old woman, drew her own unique web. She stated it wasn't a traditional web, but just as "sticky." She remarked that it was very difficult to get out of it, once trapped. Candice described the web as having a variety of layers, "which keep the center, myself, stuck." She described the pink and orange rectangles that compose the circle surrounding the star (herself) as an uncomfortable and confining type of prison. "It is all in my mind, but still a prison." The black swirls in the rectangle encompassing the pink and orange circle represent all of the problems that keep her stuck. Upon closer inspection, this shape looks like a Band-Aid™. The Band-Aid shape might represent Candice's past attempts to patch up areas of her life that have been problematic. She would try to discuss her issues with others but give up quickly, as soon as she felt pressured or too anxious. She avoided conflict at all costs. Some of Candice's problems include financial issues (owing much more money than she earns), troubles with her boyfriend of three years (he doesn't want to get married and she does), work issues (she will probably be laid off soon because of budget cuts) and relationship issues with her parents (they dislike her boyfriend and pressure her to end that relationship). The black triangles sticking out from the Band-Aid shape represent her "anger," and the circular rainbow-like shapes on the periphery of the mandala represent hope for better times. Candice remarked that her inability to do anything about her problems keeps her frozen. When asked, she stated she didn't know how long she'd be in the web, but that her past determination might help her get out eventually.

Figure 18
Mandala illustrated in the color insert

Joy

Materials: Drawing paper, paper plates, markers, paints, brushes, oil pastels, and crayons.

Procedure: Clients fill in the circle with shapes, figures, and designs that represent bliss.

Discussion: Participants explore the joy in life, and the people, places, and things that bring happiness and contentment.

Figure 19

A 66-year-old client named Eli, diagnosed with schizoaffective disorder, painted his distinctive interpretation of joy. Eli remarked that he is pleased because he has two good friends, a nice home, good food, and lots of cigarettes to smoke in his yard when he arrives home from program. He expressed happiness with his routine, which included eating in a restaurant two days a week and visiting the local Dunkin Doughnuts™, pharmacy, and bank at least once a week. He didn't like cleaning his house, but accepted it as part of his daily schedule. When asked about the mandala, Eli mentioned that the happy face he painted is not his face, although he did say he felt "good." He related it to his best friend Jim. When asked about Jim's expression, Eli remarked that Jim is happy because his friends like him and he will smoke cigarettes later today. Eli stepped outside the box because, without direction, he chose to fill in the background of the mandala with red paint and black outlined stars. He stated the stars are a gift for Jim.

Mandaloodle[2]

Materials: Markers, pen, and ink.

Procedure: The mandaloodle is a mandala/doodle. It is a circle filled with a variety of shapes, lines, and figures that connect and blend together to create a personal design. Most of the lines and shapes tend to be small and detailed. The mandaloodle can be created with colors but they are usually black and white. In this way the artist can readily follow the flow of the design. There is no right or wrong way to create a mandaloodle because the idea is to allow your design to evolve by connecting the lines and shapes in any way you choose. If you are not satisfied with one shape another may overlap or be joined in such a way to change the original form into something else. The mandaloodle represents change and the flow of life. It demonstrates how we can continue to form new ideas and increase creativity in our life. We can make lemonade out of lemons and transform/reinvent ourselves as our circumstances change. The focus of the mandaloodle is to be in the moment, to be mindful and let "our thoughts roll."

Discussion: Explore the unique symbols, shapes, and designs. Encourage participants to share how they felt creating the mandaloodle and the way it reflects their personality, mood, and experiences.

Figure 20

A woman in her 40s named Sophia designed this mandaloodle. Sophia was challenged with bipolar disorder that was presently under control. Sophia was a short, stocky, pleasant woman who enjoyed art and was able to focus on drawing and painting. Her self-esteem was improving and she was regaining a healthy equilibrium and zest for life. Sophia was delighted to work on this type of mandala. She enjoyed the freedom of expression and the idea that she didn't have to be concerned with the overall design. She was able to just let her thoughts and marker flow. She started in the center of the mandala and worked her way outwards. Sophia hummed and tapped her foot as she was drawing; she seemed to be having a lot of fun. Sophia was pleased with the outcome. When asked to describe the mandala she began, "I like the shapes and the wiggly lines; I also like the dots and straight lines. It's funny how they all come together to make a design." Upon further observation she mentioned that the center was her favorite part because "It looks like a flower and it's safe."

She remarked she liked the lines growing out of the flower, as well as the wavy shapes surrounding it. "The mandala is moving; it's like it's dancing." When asked if the mandaloodle represented her in any way she stated that she is similar to her design because she is very complicated and has many moods. Sophia remarked that she can be calm, but sometimes she feels out of control and needs assistance. She liked that the lines were contained within in the circle.

She mentioned she enjoyed using the markers because she didn't have to make decisions about which colors to use, and she liked the effect of a black and white design. She stated she couldn't believe she could create something so attractive. Sophia labeled some of the wavy lines with the dots on top of them "friendly worms." She was excited to keep drawing these mandaloodles and keep a mandaloodle journal.

Patterns

Materials: Paper plates, drawing paper, markers, oil pastels, and crayons.

Procedure: Explore the meaning of the word pattern (a design or arrangement that repeats) and show examples of patterns using magazine photos of clothes, drapery, wallpaper, and furniture. Point to various designs in client's clothing. Suggest that participants create a pattern design of their choice within the mandala.

Discussion: Examine balance, change, and life patterns. Explore how each person's life patterns are reflected in their artwork. For example, is their work balanced or off-balanced, colorful or dull, simple or complicated? Encourage participants to examine if their repeated behaviors, choices, and attitudes help them develop and grow or keep them stuck.

Figure 21
Mandala illustrated in the color insert

Art, a 68-year-old man, created a strong, yellow, orange, and black patterned mandala. He related the pattern to what was happening in his life. He stated there were many changes taking place, and he was not pleased with most of them. The black zigzag lines represented his displeasure. The wavy, double lined shape with black spikes, placed on a slight angle through the mandala, represented Art's depression and annoyance about having to sell his house and move into a smaller condominium. He said he could not take care of a large house anymore, but hated the idea of leaving it after living in it for 40 years. He also didn't like the idea of having to ask permission to plant flowers or bushes in front of his own home. He had always been his own boss and being part of a condominium community meant having to conform to the standards of the community association. The smaller orange and black zigzags represented illness (a bout with prostate cancer), retirement (after 35 years working as an accountant) and his son moving with his family to a different state. A lot was happening at once, and Art felt he was losing control of his life. He wanted things to stay the same but knew that was not reality. When asked to describe what he thought of the mandala he remarked it looked like it was being sliced in different places and this is exactly how he felt. The continuity and flow of his life had changed and he felt this change profoundly.

My favorite things

Materials: Drawing paper, markers, oil pastels, and crayons.

Procedure: Suggest that clients fill in their mandala with drawings and symbols of people, places, possessions, memories, ideas, and feelings that they cherish.

Discussion: Group members discuss what is valuable to them and what helps them enjoy life. Positive thinking and gratitude is focused upon.

Dark and light

Materials: Paper plates, drawing paper, markers, oil pastels, and crayons.

Procedure: Participants fill in one side of the mandala with dark colors and the other side with light colors.

Discussion: Explore the dark side and bright side of one's personality and/or life. Examine if one side dominates the other.

A new beginning

Materials: Drawing paper, markers, crayons, and oil pastels.

Procedure: Suggest that clients utilize various images, shapes, lines, and color to represent what a new beginning, a new start at life, would look like.

Discussion: Explore thoughts about the symbolism and associated feelings. Discuss how one's life would be similar or different in the future. Examine new coping skills and ways of thinking and relating to others. Discuss how a new beginning would affect self-esteem, mood and behavior.

Maze

Materials: Drawing paper, markers, oil pastels, crayons, and paper plates.

Procedure: Suggest clients draw a puzzle/maze within the circle and fill it in with color and/or shapes.

Discussion: Clients share the difficulty or simplicity of their maze and ways in which the maze relates to their life and/or current circumstances. Explore where the clients would be in the maze, and if applicable, the length of time they have been in it, and the approximate amount of time until they exit it.

Hope

Materials: Paper, oil pastels, markers, and crayons.

Procedure: Clients draw or paint what hope means to them. Suggest they create images of expectations, wishes, goals, and desires.

Discussion/goals: Explore the symbols presented and their significance. Support clients to maintain a positive attitude while striving to achieve good mental health and recovery from depression and anxiety. Help clients identify realistic goals.

Past/present

Materials: Paper plates, drawing paper, markers, oil pastels, and crayons.

Procedure: Fill in half of the circle with symbols representing the past and the other half of the circle with symbols representing the present.

Discussion: Discuss ways in which past experiences have influenced present mood and behaviors. Reminisce about positive experiences and strengths. Examine which period of time clients were the most content, and explore ways to attain similar satisfaction in the present.

In control/out of control

Materials: Paper plates, drawing paper, markers, oil pastels, and crayons.

Procedure: Fill part of the circle with shapes, lines, figures, and/or designs that represent being in control and fill in the rest of the mandala with shapes, lines, etc. that represent being out of control.

Discussion: Explore the differences and/or similarities in the images and colors. How does the mandala reflect one's personality and behavior? Explore ways in which control issues were focused upon in the artwork. Examine how control issues affect relationships, mood, feelings, communication skills, and behaviors.

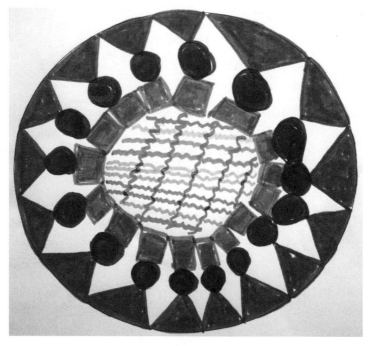

Figure 22
Mandala illustrated in the color insert

A woman in her 20s designed this engaging, detailed mandala. She stated, "I didn't have a plan in mind when I started, so it became me letting go, keeping in mind to represent in control and out of control. The effortless parts came to represent being out of control. The parts that required a steady hand and a pattern came to represent being in control. I noticed those parts seem to have darker colors... interesting." This individual found it easier to create the center, out of control, design. She related the colors and wavy lines to feeling hyper and energized when she's out of control, and more somber and sober (darker colors, patterns created as the circle moves outward) when in control. It is noteworthy that this client was trying to structure her life, working towards overcoming addiction issues that were adversely affecting her health, close relationships, marriage, and job.

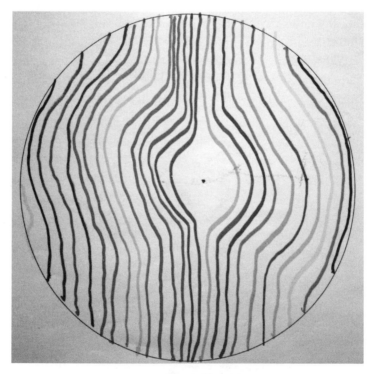

Figure 23

A young man in his 20s, named Chris, called this mandala "Nothing." At first he remarked that it had no significance. As other clients began sharing their thoughts about their mandalas he began to share a little more. Chris remarked that he feels dizzy when he stares at the mandala too long. "The lines aren't balanced; one side has more lines than the other." He stated that the dot in the center represented him. "I am like that tiny dot." He went on to say that he felt insignificant in his life. "I didn't go to college and I have a shitty job; I don't like my girlfriend very much and I don't have many friends." He saw himself being surrounded by a life (all the lines) that was scary and difficult. "Why can't things just be easy; why does everything have to be so hard?" When asked, he remarked that although the mandala appears in control; he feels out of control. He felt his life was out of control. One client asked him if he was hiding, and Chris replied that he might be. The other group members saw the dot as "hiding out," in between all the other lines that were protecting it. Chris agreed with this observation and then stated that if the dot (himself) moves he doesn't know what would happen. He was able to acknowledge that he keeps in control by not working to change his life. He is safe even though he is dissatisfied. Chris agreed with his peers that the unknown could be very scary. He was supported to think about the benefits of taking healthy risks and making healthy changes in his life.

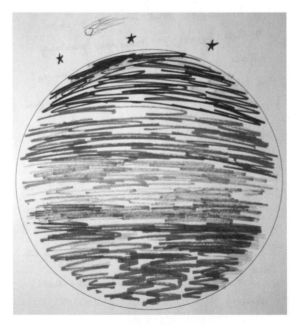

Figure 24

Jim, a very intelligent man in his 30s, diagnosed with schizophrenia, drew a colorful mandala that appears to be a planet. Jim is a computer whiz and a chess master. He is sweet, social, and likable. The mandala was drawn with a quick hand; the colors are filled in with a scribbled style, but they were chosen carefully. The quickness of the lines may represent Jim's thoughts, which raced at times. Jim's associations to the mandala represent his disorganization, delusional, and sometimes tangential, thinking. Three small stars were placed on top of the mandala. Jim wrote, "Earth and its inhabitants are in control. A fluid dynamic of homeostasis maintaining balance for as long as the earth survives, provides a stable life cycle. The heavens and space is beyond control at this point in time. We remain at the mercy of the elements beyond our blue marble. For whatever the universe may create, it can take away. We never know when the delicate environment, in which we live, will be irreversibly upset. Live like everyday is your last and you'll never be at the whim of celestial chaos." He titled the work "Space Cadet."

Problem/solution

Materials: Drawing paper, markers, oil pastels, and crayons.

Procedure: Illustrate a problem on one side of the mandala and then draw the solution on the other side.

Discussion: Focus on problem solving and self-awareness. Identify worries and concerns, and work on ways to deal with them in an effective and healthy manner.

Healing hand

Materials: Drawing paper, markers, crayons, and oil pastels.

Procedure: Have clients trace one hand inside the mandala. Ask them to fill in the hand with healing shapes, colors, and symbols. Suggest they fill in the background with colors that represent comfort and support.

Discussion: Explore what clients need to recover from their illness. Examine ways in which individuals can self-soothe, e.g. positive self-talk, good sleep, hygiene, eating nutritiously.

In the moment

Materials: Drawing paper, markers, oil pastels, pastels, and crayons.

Procedure: Clients choose one color that best represents their current mood and uses it to fill in the circle with figures and shapes that also represent their current mood.

Discussion: Explore and identify mood and feelings, and methods of expression. Ask clients, "How does your mood affect your actions, reactions, behavior, and relationships?"

Gratitude

Materials: Drawing paper, markers, crayons, and oil pastels.

Procedure: Instruct participants to fill in the mandala with symbols and images representing things they are thankful for in their life. Suggestions may include: family, friends, love, health, sunrise and sunsets, flowers, trees, nature, rainbows, birds, puppies, babies, food, electronics, books, music, art, etc.

Discussion: Encourage clients to use the mandala as a tool that will remind them to think in a more positive manner. Explore the wonderful aspects of each individual's life, his achievements, prized possessions, loves, comforts, and interests. Discuss the simple pleasures of life, such as holding hands with a partner, watching a child laugh, or picking colorful flowers on a bright spring afternoon.

Dream symbols

Materials: Drawing paper, markers, and oil pastels.

Procedure: Have participants represent various aspects of significant dreams in the mandala. This would include symbols, figures, and an unusual or extraordinary environment. Examples might include:

a narrow, winding highway, a huge black bear, a deceased relative, etc. The idea is to take symbols of various dreams and include all of them in one mandala.

Discussion: Explore the individual symbols and then examine how they are similar and/or different from one another. Look for patterns, connections, meanings, and the way all the symbols work to create a complete design.

Figure 25

Greg, a 30-year-old male challenged with schizophrenia, represented a nightmare he "has every night." The mandala consists of symbols representing his mother beating him and his associated terror. He shared that as a child he was frequently beaten and verbally abused. His mother was the prime culprit, but she would occasionally bring male and female friends to the house and they would also berate him and hit him, sometimes with a broomstick. The arrow over the face (right side of mandala) represents the fear and pain he endured and still experiences in his dreams. On the right hand side is a figure holding a sort of tree branch, which represents his beatings. The words "You is mine" is written under the face. His mother would say this to him as she hit him. The tree next to the distorted face represented "lightning and torture."

There are a few small hearts included that symbolize the "love he has in his heart" for his "friends, girlfriend, and a lot of people in my neighborhood." Although Greg added the hearts as a love symbol, he was recently in a heated argument with another man and felt angry enough to severely harm him. He stated he would have killed him if his uncle hadn't intervened and pulled him away. Greg was able to acknowledge that removing himself from the situation was a wise move because he didn't want to go to jail. He remarked that he has anger issues "sometimes." Greg was very willing to share this nightmare and experiences with his peers because he "felt comfortable."

Truth

Materials: Drawing paper, markers, crayons, and oil pastels.

Procedure: Clients write the word truth in the center of the mandala or the group leader prints out the word from Microsoft Word™ and distributes to each participant. The participants glue the word onto the middle of the mandala. Instruct clients to fill in the space surrounding the word "truth" in a manner that represents what is true and meaningful in their life and/or what truth means to them.

Discussion: Examine how being genuine and living an authentic life affects happiness, mood, and behavior. Explore whether clients are trying to please others or living the life they desire.

Figure 26

Nan, a woman in her 50s, placed "Truth and Justice" in the center of the circle. She chose to add the "and Justice" for emphasis. Flowers that seem alive and moving with a slight slant to the left side of the mandala surround the words. The flowers are filled in with bold colors: red, blue, orange, and purple. Nan related the theme and vividness of the flowers to the importance of being true to oneself and not allowing others to dictate "what you do, what you should wear, or how you should live your life." Nan stated that she always listened to what others said and never really felt content. She went to college, married when she was supposed to, had children, and did all her wifely duties. Her house was neat and clean, and she participated in all the motherly things like the parent teacher organizations. Each night she prepared the home cooked meals her husband demanded of her. Her husband decided how much money they would spend, where they would go on vacation, and who their friends would be. He even decided which clothes she would wear when they went out to dinner. She cut her hair short when he decided she'd look more sophisticated with a new hairdo. Nan spent her life doing for others and ignoring her own needs. Through therapy and hard work she began gaining self-esteem and learning that she was never true to herself. This unhealthy attitude and life style significantly contributed to her anxiety and depression. Her plan was to begin focusing on her own needs, desires, and goals, while continuing to gain self-awareness and assertiveness in her marital relationship.

Time of day

Materials: Drawing paper, markers, crayons, and oil pastels.

Procedure: Participants divide their mandala into four parts: Morning, afternoon, evening, and night. They may decide the size of the section according to the way they feel during that particular time of day. For instance, if they feel happier and have energy in the morning, but feel depleted and depressed in the evening they may draw the morning segment larger than the evening segment. Next have participants fill in the mandala with symbols, colors, designs, and figures that represent their feelings during the different parts of the day.

Discussion: Explore the time of day that participants feel the best and the worst. Examine what occurs during those periods of time. Examine how the person feels, what he does and what his self-talk is at the time. Discuss ways to structure time so that having something healthy to focus upon lifts one's mood. Examples may include working on a hobby, exercising, drawing, reading, or calling a friend or family member.

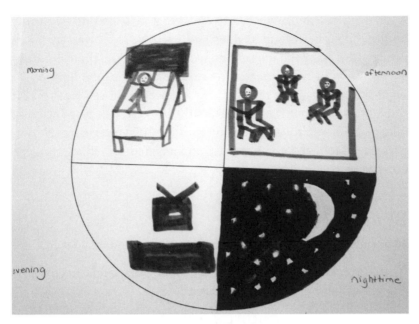

Figure 27

Lawrence, a 27-year-old man challenged with disabling anxiety, represented each segment of the mandala with an image. The first segment drawn, a person lying in bed, symbolizes the morning. Lawrence stated he has a lot of difficulty getting up in the morning; he always wants to sleep at least an extra half hour. He shared that sometimes he pulls the covers over his head and ignores the alarm. He has been late to program on numerous occasions and knows this is an important issue to work on. The afternoon, depicted by three people sitting in chairs, symbolizes his work in the psychiatric program. He is the small figure in the middle. Lawrence remarked that he likes sharing his feelings and "getting things out." He stated he enjoys art therapy, even though he believes he is not creative. Lawrence remarked he likes sharing his artwork and listening to other's observations and questions. A television and a couch represent evening. Lawrence stated that he eats dinner with his father every night and they watch television programs together; they often go to a local diner instead of eating at home. He mentioned he enjoys this time with his father and appreciates their close relationship. His father is very supportive and serves as a role model for him. Nighttime is when he sleeps but that is often a problem. Lawrence explained that he wakes up frequently during the night, feeling anxious and stressed. He leaves his blinds open so he can see the stars and sometimes the moon; there is a street lamp in front of his house. Lawrence stated he finds the light of the night sky soothing. He revealed that lately he has been having a lot of nightmares about friends and family. He is fearful to go to sleep because he doesn't want to keep repeating this experience. He was encouraged to practice mindfulness and meditation, and to journal in order to help calm his nerves.

Beginning/end

Materials: Drawing paper, markers, oil pastels, and crayons.

Procedure: Participants create a design within the circle that includes a clear starting point and ending point.

Discussion: Clients share the significance of the beginning and ending of the drawing, and how the beginning and ending points affect the completed design. Explore how the mandalas may relate to each individual's "beginning and ending." This may be interpreted in any way the client desires. Examples may include the beginning of therapy and thoughts about its completion, the beginning and ending of illness, or the beginning of life and thoughts about the future.

Profiles

Materials: Drawing paper, markers, oil pastels, and crayons.

Procedure: Clients are asked to draw two profiles facing each other within the circle. Templates may be used (clients trace the outlines) if desired. The profiles may be male or female, human or animal.

Discussion: Clients are asked to relate the profiles to people or things of significance in their life. Ask them to explore the strength of the faces, characteristics, colors used, and expressions. Examine if the profiles appear equal or if one stands out in some way.

Explore if they are male or female, human or animal. Encourage participants to create a story about the profiles if they are not able to associate them to themselves or their life in some way. Discuss various sides of our personality and the idea of having "two faces" (our inner and outer face—what we share with the world and what we hide) or being "two faced" (hypocritical).

Spirituality

Materials: Drawing paper, markers, crayons, and oil pastels.

Procedure: Participants are asked to fill in the mandala with symbols, colors, and shapes representing what spirituality means to them. Clarify that spirituality can take on various meanings. It may include religion, art nature, attitude, an appreciation of the world, love of people, etc.

Discussion: Discuss what spirituality means to group members. Explore how spirituality affects mood, behavior, attitude, self-esteem, and self-awareness. Examine feelings elicited from each sacred mandala.

Path to recovery

Materials: Drawing paper, markers, oil pastels, and crayons.

Procedure: Have clients draw a representation of what their path to recovery might look like. Suggest they use objects such as mountains, trees, flowers, houses, cars, signs, crossroads, people, bumps, stones, and detours.

Discussion/goals: Discussion focuses on the length of the path and what is placed on it. For instance: Is the path bumpy, smooth, and/or winding? Are there obstacles on the road? Is the path full of flowers and trees or potholes and swamps? Clients explore goals, methods to attain them, assessment of the amount of therapeutic work ahead, and attitude toward recovery.

Figure 28

A man in his 40s, named Samuel, drew a road leading to his home, which represented his personal pathway to recovery. Samuel was a recovering addict and was presently living in a halfway house. His hope and goal was to be allowed back home and to be forgiven by his wife. He stated he missed his wife and children greatly. While he was on drugs he was very irresponsible and negligent to his family. He would sometimes spend grocery and mortgage money on drugs. He was in danger of losing his home to the bank because of his cocaine habit and recklessness. His wife gave him an ultimatum, which was to attend a program and get help or she would divorce him. He was terrified of losing his family and home, describing his wife and home as beautiful and comforting. Samuel berated himself for "being so stupid" and almost losing it all. He drew a cart on the road, and flowers, grass, trees, and two tiny sheds bordering it. There is a sun in the sky, two clouds, and two birds (he has two children). Samuel stated he felt pleased looking at the images and wished he would be accepted at home as soon as possible. When asked where his present position would be on his road, he replied, "Where the cart is located, at least *now* I'm on the road." He hoped to get closer to the door in the next few weeks.

Passion mandala

Materials: Drawing paper, markers, oil pastels, and crayons.

Procedure: Suggest that clients draw things they are passionate about and/or use colors and shapes to represent passion. Examples may include children/grandchildren, pets, hobbies, work, art, volunteer positions, sports such as golf, etc.

Discussion/goals: Discussion focuses on the importance of having a passion and/or a purpose in life. Explain the benefits:

- Individuals are generally more positive.

- They often have higher self-esteem and less depression.

- They have more energy.

- They are more likely to fight off disease and illness.

- They live longer.

Figure 29
Mandala illustrated in the color insert

A 39-year-old female named Kyra created a colorful, very passionate mandala. The bright orange sun is outlined in yellow and represented Kyra's love of life, "before depression." She stated she had been very passionate in many areas of her life. She believed she was a very good wife and mother, going over and beyond what a typical mother would do. She often sewed her children's clothes, baked treats, and played with them when they were younger. She had a variety of hobbies, such as cooking, which she felt strongly about, and friends she loved. Kyra remarked that she went "above and beyond at work." The blue wave in the mandala represented her highs and lows associated with her bipolar disorder, and the brown shape above the waves symbolized her gloom, which she was experiencing at the moment. The ominous looking green shape on the left hand side of the mandala represented her fear of being taken over by her illness. "It is like a monster takes over me." She stated when she has her highs and lows she is like a different person. She expressed fear of the green hand-like shape. Kyra remarked that her moods vacillate so she never knows how she'll be feeling on any given day. This makes it difficult for her to make plans and to lead a balanced life. Kyra enjoyed the structure of the mandala, stating she needs more structure when she is out of control.

Culture

Materials: Drawing paper, markers, oil pastels, and crayons.

Procedure: Ask clients to think about various aspects of their culture. Suggest they draw symbols representing their culture/religion, traditions, spirituality, etc. Examples include: a menorah, Christmas tree, Buddha, cross, rosary beads, Seder dinners, etc.

Discussion/goals: Explore the impact that culture has on attitudes, relationships, identity, and self-worth. Goals include sharing, socialization, and self-awareness. Speaking about one's customs and background often increases self-esteem and discussion among seniors. It frequently elicits memories of joyful family events and gatherings. Many seniors find prayer and religion to be a major coping skill.

Rescue mandala

Materials: Drawing paper, markers, oil pastels, and crayons

Procedure: Group members draw images; shapes and designs that represent methods they can utilize to *come to their own rescue* (help themselves to recover from worry, illness, fear, anxiety and loneliness, etc.). A bright background filled with energizing colors may be included.

Discussion: Explore independence; examine the theme of "doing for yourself" (not always looking to others for assistance). Discuss ways to avoid relapse and become healthier and happier using various methods such as being medication compliant, exercising, joining groups, structuring one's time, eating nutritious food, getting enough sleep, finding hobbies, buying one's own flowers, and celebrating one's own birthday, taking oneself to a restaurant, thinking positively, and honoring oneself. Examine methods to avoid being a victim, such as being self-aware and being cognizant of warning signs of depression and intense anxiety such as isolating from others, experiencing poor memory and concentration, irritability, panic attacks, and not sleeping well.

Love mandala

Materials: Drawing paper, markers, oil pastels, and crayons.

Procedure: Ask clients to fill the circle with things they love. For example: family members, coffee, chocolate, food, books, a summer day, etc.

Discussion/goals: Discussion focuses on the items depicted, their size and significance. Goals include assessing what is important and meaningful in one's life and positive thinking.

Gareth, a young man in his mid 20s challenged with bipolar disorder and addiction issues, designed this colorful mandala. The two figures at the bottom of the page represent his ex-girlfriend Tiffany and him. He is smiling and Tiffany is frowning. "That is because she is never satisfied with anything." Gareth mentioned that he really loved and still loves her, but she is "bad for my self-esteem and she is very

Figure 30
Mandala illustrated in the color insert

self-centered." She constantly wanted Gareth to take her to fancy restaurants and bars, and buy her jewelry and clothes even though he only received a small disability check once a month. "She is very selfish." He continued to say that even though she has a variety of "bad qualities" she is still fun to be with and she is gorgeous. Gareth is experiencing conflicting feelings because his parents and psychiatrist insisted he end the relationship for his own good. He was spending all of his time with Tiffany and she was causing him much stress. He needed to focus on his own health and recovery. In addition, she was drinking and smoking marijuana. He had been alcohol and drug free for a month and his parents were afraid of relapse. Gareth mentioned that he still dreams about Tiffany and wishes he could see her, but he knows it's for the best to stay away. He fears she will find someone new soon and share her latest status on Facebook™. Gareth said he would be devastated if he found out she was in a relationship, but refused to give up his Facebook page or block her from his page. The rows of colors on top of the two figures in the mandala represent different moods Gareth is currently experiencing. The top brown represents negativity and the middle yellow and pink symbolize his hope that he meets someone new in the future "who will be better for me."

Spiral mandala I

Materials: Paper, pastels, crayons, and markers.

Procedure: Demonstrate how to draw a spiral. Suggest that clients create a design within the circle using spirals of varying sizes and colors.

Discussion/goals: Discussion focuses on the connection made between the artwork and the client's emotional state. For instance, does the client feel like he is spiraling upward, inward, or downward? Does he feel caught in a spiral, confused, going around in circles? Ask clients, "In what way is your life like a spiral?" Goals include identifying and expressing emotions and feelings.

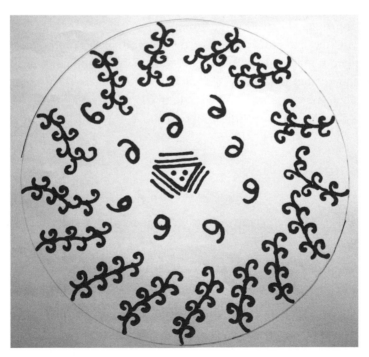

Figure 31

Olivia, a woman in her 30s, challenged with bipolar disorder, drew a series of small spirals and "spiral flowers" to represent family members. She placed her parents in the center of the mandala (the small triangle with the three dots in it), and eight spirals surrounding the triangle represent her brothers and sisters. She was the youngest of eight children. The center spiral to the right represents Olivia. Olivia remarked that she had a wonderful childhood, full of fun and adventure. She was never lonely or bored because there was always someone to play with. Her parents would spoil her because she was the youngest and very demanding at times. Olivia remarked that she had to be loud and aggressive or else she would not be heard in such a large household. She relayed a story where she purposely spilled a full container of milk on the floor and pretended it accidentally slipped off the table so she could get her mother's attention. Another time she faked falling down the steps so her mother would coddle her. Unfortunately this unhealthy manipulative behavior stuck with Olivia through adulthood, culminating in an unsuccessful suicide attempt to gain sympathy and attention.

The tree-like spirals on the border of the mandala represent a large extended family consisting of many aunts, uncles and cousins. Olivia mentioned that her family supports her and helps keep her morale up; they are very close. When asked to critique her work, Olivia viewed the mandala as "full of life and love, but a little scrambled."

Balance

Materials: Drawing paper, pastels, crayons, and markers.

Procedure: Direct clients to create a balanced design using various shapes.

Discussion: Support clients to relate their artwork to how they balance different aspects of their lives. Examine if the mandala designs are centered, scattered, etc. Questions to ask include: Do you find you are able to balance your family life, work, responsibilities, and social obligations? Are you off balance at the moment? How can you regain and/or maintain your balance? Goals include identifying methods to gain control of one's life.

Positive images

Materials: Drawing paper, pastels, markers, oil pastels, and crayons.

Procedure: Suggest that group members think of as many positive images as they can, and represent them in any way they wish within the circle.

Discussion/goals: Discussion focuses on the images and the positive feelings associated with the images. The relationship between thinking optimistically and better mental and physical health is explored.

Scribble design mandalas

Materials: Paper, pastels, crayons, markers, and paper plate.

Procedure: Direct clients to outline a circle with a black marker or crayon using a paper plate as a template. Suggest they use the black marker/crayon to make a large scribble within the mandala, taking up all or most of the space. Then ask clients to fill in the scribble design with color. When the drawing is completed have the clients view the mandala from all angles and see if they can find anything that looks familiar in it (a face, animal, part of an object, etc.). Next ask clients to think of a title for the picture.

Discussion/goals: Discussion focuses on what clients saw in the design and how they felt about coloring within the circular border and/or whether they even stayed within the border. Goals include projection of feelings through images, focusing, and stress reduction.

Observation

Materials: Drawing paper, markers, oil pastels, and crayons.

Procedure: Clients are asked to draw an eye in the center of the mandala, or they may cut a photo of an eye from a magazine and glue it onto the mandala. Next have participants draw what they see in their environment. Examples may include abstract symbols such as love and happiness and/or concrete objects such as flowers, birds, trees, houses, and people.

Discussion: Participants share their observations and feelings about their life and surroundings. Explore whether or not they are satisfied with what they observe and whether or not they need to expand their world and awareness.

Life flow

Materials: Drawing paper, markers, pastels, oil pastels, and crayons.

Procedure: Clients represent their life flow (progression of their life). Encourage them to represent whether their flow is gentle, smooth, strong, weak, wavy, choppy, treacherous, shallow, or deep. They may symbolize this through shape, color, line, and design.

Discussion: Explore how the designs symbolize an easy or difficult, mild or complex life. Examine how one's flow may change and vary during different life stages. Discuss ways to cope with and tame the flow if necessary.

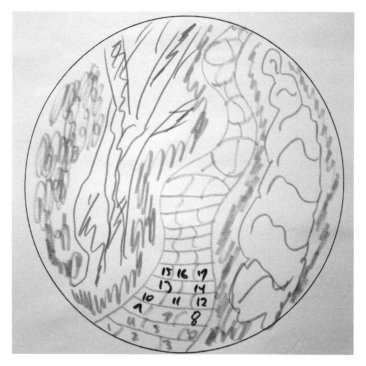

Figure 32

A brilliant man named Charles, challenged with bipolar disorder, designed his life flow. He described it as very mathematical and complicated. The road weaving through the river is flowing upwards and the numbers situated in the squares composing the road are increasing. According to the artist, they represent the challenges of life and the "difficult formulas we all have to deal with." The road and water are choppy and dangerous. Charles mentioned that he has no idea if he will survive the road. There are many obstacles on the road including a "broken tree, storms, rough winds and waves, and dark clouds." Charles took a wait and see approach, seemingly content to take one day at a time, although he felt his prospects for the future appeared dim at times.

Energy

Materials: Drawing paper, markers, oil pastels, and crayons.

Procedure: Participants represent their energy using color, line, shape, and design.

Discussion: Discussion focuses on how one's energy affects mood and activity. Observe movement and vitality in the artwork, and explore methods to increase vigor.

Present and future

Materials: Drawing paper, pastels, crayons, and markers.

Procedure: Suggest that clients draw life as it is on one side of the paper and life if "you felt well" on the other side of the paper.

Discussion/goals: Discussion focuses on exploring the obstacles individuals encounter while struggling with depression, anxiety, and other mental illness. Goals include increasing self-awareness by examining the differences between one's present circumstances and one's ideal circumstances. Implementing a plan of action toward recovery may be focused upon.

Graffiti mandala

Materials: Markers, paint, brushes, and water.

Procedure: Direct participants to fill in the circle with graffiti of any sort. As a reference point, ask clients to think of the style of graffiti they may see on trains, buses, or the side of buildings. Discuss reasons people create graffiti, some of which may include: they are often trying to focus attention on themselves or on their point of view; sometimes they are rebelling against a person, place, or thing, and sometimes they are just having fun and being mischievous.

Discussion: Examine the meaning of the graffiti drawn within the mandala. Observe how the graffiti renderings become a design and personal statement. Explore the feeling of freedom associated with expressing thoughts and feelings in an unrestricted manner.

Mandala dream catcher

Materials: Drawing paper, markers, crayons, oil pastels, paint, pencils, colored pencils, brushes, and water.

Procedure: Discuss the origin of the dream catcher: the earliest dreamcatchers, commonly called Sacred Hoops, were crafted by parents to protect their children from nightmares. Newborns were given charms that were woven in the form of spider webs to protect their dreams so their innocence would not be harmed by the tricksters of the night. The dream catcher charm would be hung from the hoop on the cradle.[3]

Next have clients draw their own unique dream catcher.

1. Create a circle within the original circle leaving about one half inch (1 cm) of space from the perimeter of the first circle to the perimeter of the second circle. This will become the frame of the dream catcher.

2. Make an equidistant vertical and then horizontal line so that the two intersect in the center of the circle.

3. In the center of the circle draw a series of petal like shapes that overlap to create the net. Include beads placed randomly on the petals.

4. Add three lines at the bottom of the circle for feathers.

5. Sketch feather shapes around the lines. Draw a shallow curved line from the top to the bottom of the line (on each side of it) to create the feather. Repeat for each feather.

6. If you like, add the binding to the ring around the mandala by filling in the ring with angled lines. This will make the ring look leather-like.

7. Fill the dream catcher with color.

Discussion: Explore dreams and daydreams that clients would like trapped in the dream catcher. Observe and discuss how each unique catcher might work for each group member. Examine how thinking positively and feeling safe helps people relax and get a better night's sleep. Discuss other methods to feel safe and secure at night.

Loss

Materials: Drawing paper, markers, crayons, and oil pastels.

Procedure: Clients fill in the mandala with shapes, images, lines, and designs that represent a loss (recent or in the past). Clarify that the loss may be a loss of abilities, a friend or loved one, a pet, a job, a marriage, a prized possession, finances, stature, home, health, etc.

Discussion: Explore the symbolism and the significance of the loss. Discuss thoughts and feelings associated with the loss and how it has affected one's mood, behavior, thoughts, feelings, attitudes and life style. Explore coping techniques such as mindfulness and stress reduction practices such as structuring one's day to keep busy, exercising, sharing with loved ones, and taking one day at a time.

Figure 33

A woman in her late 60s named Emily drew a dancer as the focal point of her mandala. The figure appears to be dancing the Hula; her arms and legs seem rubbery. She isn't wearing a top and her expression seems angry (as expressed by her black, slanted eyebrows). She is wearing a dotted type of crown and one leg is placed partly outside of the circle. Musical notes are surrounding her in and outside of the circle. The figure is drawn in light pink marker; her slanted eyebrow, crown, and one musical note is drawn in black and stand out the most. The dancer looks like she is partly on her toes and could fall easily. She appears to be leaning slightly to the right. Emily described the figure as someone unknown, "She's just some woman trying to dance." When asked if she could relate to the woman, Emily stated that she used to like dancing, but now she has arthritis and "everything hurts. I can't dance; I can hardly walk now." When asked what she thought of the woman's expression she said she was annoyed because she has no one to dance with. Emily's husband had passed away a few years ago. The emptiness of the mandala (lack of color and background) might be related to the loneliness Emily is presently experiencing, and her sense of loss. She is considering moving to an assisted living facility but hasn't made up her mind as of yet. When prompted, she remarked that she liked the pink skirt and had a similar one when she was young. She titled the work "The Hula Dancer."

Eye mandala[4]

Materials: Drawing paper, magazines, scissors, glue, markers, and crayons.

Procedure: Instruct participants to utilize the magazines provided to search for photos of eyes (varying sizes, shapes, colors, etc.). Next direct them to glue the eyes on the mandala in any way they wish to form a design. Clients may also use markers and pastels to add to the composition. Explain that the collage can be connected to the Hindu Goddess Ankamma, a guardian protector goddess. She is thought to have 1000 eyes to keep watch on her devotees wherever they went.

Discussion: Explore patterns and designs. Discuss the significance of the eyes: are they welcoming or threatening? Do they represent wisdom, or a feeling of vagueness and emptiness? Ask participants if their personality characteristics are similar to Ankamma: do they keep watch over friends and family? Do they watch over themselves? Are they self-aware?

Flower mandala: Number eight[5]

Materials: Drawing paper, markers, crayons, and oil pastels.

Procedure: Direct clients to write the number eight within the circle. They will create the eight using two large zeros, one on top of the other. In this way the eight touches the edges of the circle from top to bottom. The eights will be drawn first vertically and then horizontally in the same manner. The zeros (circles) will overlap to create a simple flower design. Ask participants to draw a very small circle in the middle of the flower to complete it. Lastly, have clients fill in the flower with color, lines, and patterns.

Discussion: Explore ways in which the number eight is significant in various cultures and religions. Discuss thoughts about creating the flower from the number eight and examine what else could be created from the number (examples may include the head and body of a person or a fish). Ask clients if they can relate to the number in any way (for example eight good friends, winning a prize using that number, born on the eighth of the month, eight cousins, nieces and nephews or eight grandchildren, etc.).

Present the following information:

- The number eight has significance in many cultures and religions.

- The Dharmacakra, a Buddhist symbol, has eight spokes.

- The Jewish religious rite of brit milah (commonly known as circumcision) is held on a baby boy's eighth day of life.

- Hanukkah is an eight-day Jewish holiday that starts on the 25th day of Kislev.

- Shemini Atzeret (Hebrew: "Eighth Day of Assembly") is a one-day Jewish holiday immediately following the seven-day holiday of Sukkot.

- In Islam, it is the number of angels carrying The Holy Throne of Allah in the heavens.

- The Eight Immortals are Chinese demigods.

- In Wicca, there are eight Sabbats, festivals, seasons, or spokes in the Wheel of the Year.

- In Hinduism it's the number of wealth, abundance. The Goddess Lakshmi has eightfold forms. There are eight nidhis—seats of wealth. Also, there are eight Guardians of the directions.

- Eight (八, pinyin bā) is considered a lucky number in Chinese culture because it sounds like the word meaning to generate wealth (发, Pinyin: fā). Property with the number 8 may be valued greatly by Chinese.

- Eight (八, hachi) is also considered a lucky number in Japanese culture, but the reason is different from that in Chinese culture. Eight gives an idea of growing prosperous, because the letter (八) broadens gradually.

- In the Middle Ages, 8 was the number of "unmoving" stars in the sky, and symbolized the perfection of incoming planetary energy.

- It is 7 plus 1. Hence it is the number specially associated with resurrection and regeneration, and the beginning of a new era or order.

- According to the Bible, eight has a special meaning for God, as He chose the eighth day to mark the beginning of the new week. Everything that has a new beginning in the Bible has the number eight associated with it.

Growth

Materials: Drawing paper, markers, oil pastels, and crayons.

Procedure: Participants draw a plant, flower, or tree displaying its root system. A background may be added.

Discussion: Explore the size of the plant, the colors used, and the size and dimensions of the roots. Ask questions such as:

- Are the roots long and thick or short and thin?

- Have the roots been growing for a long time or are they newly formed?

- Are the roots strong and well entrenched in the ground, or weak and shallow?

- Do they keep the plant in place or is the plant wobbly?

- Can you identify with the root system depicted (in terms of being "rooted" in your life)?

- Have the roots been nourished over the years?

- What do the roots need to flourish (meaning what do you need to grow and prosper)?

Recovery[6]

Materials: Drawing paper, markers, oil pastels, and crayons.

Procedure: Instruct participants to draw a smaller circle within the larger one. In the smaller circle have them depict a physical or psychological problem that they are experiencing. Suggest they surround the problem with colors, shapes, designs, and images they perceive as healing.

Discussion: Observe the size, shape, and intensity of the illness represented. Examine the environment surrounding it and discuss how the environment affects it (perhaps protects it, invades it, or destroys it). Discuss methods to work towards recovery.

Bird mandala[7]

Materials: Templates of birds of various sizes, drawing paper, markers, oil pastels, crayons, and colored pencils.

Procedure: Clients fill in the circle with as many birds as they please. They may create a pattern or place the birds in a random manner. Backgrounds of shapes, colors, leaves, and flowers may be added.

Discussion: Observe the composition, designs, and colors utilized. Discuss each client's association to the birds. Explore related themes such as nature, beauty (associated with colorful feathers and sweet chirping), freedom (associated with flying), and nesting (associated with family and connectedness).

Rainbow

Materials: Drawing paper, oil pastels, crayons, and markers.

Procedure: Clients are asked to draw a rainbow of colors within the circle.

Discussion: Discussion may focus on emotions, energy, thoughts, and attitude towards recovery. The rainbow may be compared to the client's feelings of hope and strength. For example: Is it a large, colorful rainbow or a small weakly drawn design?

Guilt[8]

Materials: Drawing paper, markers, oil pastels, and crayons.

Procedure: Group participants fill in the circle with images, shapes, colors, and words that represent a time in their life they have felt guilty, or what guilt feels or looks like to them.

Discussion: Explore the personal meanings of the mandalas. Discuss what guilt feels like and how it affects self-esteem and one's attitude towards life. Examine the few positive and the many negative consequences of guilt. Explore reasons why group members might hold on to their guilt. Ask individuals if they are ready to let go of any remorse they might be experiencing, and examine methods to let it go.

A place in my heart

Materials: Drawing paper, markers, crayons, oil pastels, paint, brushes, and colored pencils.

Procedure: Instruct clients to draw or paint a person, pet, or item that holds a special place in their heart. Have them include a background.

Discussion: Ask clients to discuss the significance of the person, animal, or object, and how it is represented in the mandala. Discuss what makes it special and meaningful. The following questions may be explored:

- Is the person or pet still a part of your life?

- Does he/it help you cope with life?

- Has he/it affected your self-esteem?

- What do you/will you remember most about this person, pet, or object?

- What has he/it taught you about life or about yourself?

- If you could say anything to him/it now, what would you say?

Figure 34

A 70-year-old woman named Belinda drew an abstract portrait of her dog, Amanda. Amanda had recently died at the age of 12; she was a gray poodle. Belinda stated she drew the dog in an abstract manner because she couldn't bear to draw her realistically, "It would have been too painful." She said she was having a very difficult time getting over the death of her beloved dog. She remarked that Amanda was an important member of the family. "She often slept with my husband and myself, sometimes taking up an awful lot of room on the bed. My husband and I would argue because he thought she should be in her crate, but I insisted she sleep where she was most comfortable. She was my baby. Amanda went with us wherever we went. She would hop in the car as soon as we opened the garage door; she loved to take car rides. She would bark softly and seemed to have a grin on her face when the car would start." Belinda stated,

"I think I loved Amanda more than my own children. I would never tell anyone else, but since this is therapy… She was my third child; I adored her. I just can't believe I will never see her again. I didn't even know she was sick. She just looked depressed for a few days and then she was dead—just like that!"

Belinda focused on Amanda's eyes in the mandala. They are large, brown, sad looking eyes. "The last few days of her life she seemed depressed, I thought maybe she didn't like the colder weather or her new dog food; she loved people food. I think she was trying to tell me she was sick by using her big sad eyes; I just didn't get it. I can be stupid at times. If only she could have told me she didn't feel well." Belinda went on, "I will never forget her eyes; I have had dreams where she is staring at me; I wake up shaking."

Belinda also included bright colors in the background "to represent the joy and color she brought into our lives. She was an amazingly sweet and good-tempered dog. She had a teeny bark, sort of like a 'gruff, gruff,' when visitors approached. The bark only lasted a minute and it was so cute. She wouldn't have hurt a fly. She only wanted to be petted and loved." A rainbow is also included "to represent the hope that she is in the sky, in a sort of dog heaven." Belinda stated that the mandala was difficult to draw, but comforting. "It gave me a way to express my feelings about Amanda. I expressed my love for her." She remarked that she would frame the mandala and hang it in her bedroom as a tribute to the dog.

Create a utopia

Materials: Drawing paper, markers, crayons, and oil pastels.

Procedure: Discuss the meaning of the word utopia. Encourage clients to close their eyes, relax, and visualize what their own private paradise would be like. Invite group members to explore this special place; to observe the lifestyles, colors, smells, architecture, and weather there. When clients have had sufficient time visualizing this environment ask them to draw a picture within the circle illustrating their utopia.

Discussion: Individuals are encouraged to share goals, wishes, and dreams. Methods of attaining a satisfying life are explored.

Figure 35

A very sweet 41-year-old man named Bill, diagnosed with bipolar disorder, drew his version of utopia. The focus of the mandala is on a rocket ship that "has landed on another planet." Bill remarked that he'd like to live on a planet that is beautiful and serene, a planet that is not polluted and where there is no crime, and a place where everyone is kind and nice to each other. There would be no prejudice and no one would be hungry or financially strapped in this world. He stated the weather would be warm and sunny, and there would always be lots of large, shining stars in the sky. He remarked that it would be easy to take trips in the rocket ship to visit planets near by "for vacation." Bill added two people skateboarding to represent the fun most people would have each day in his world. He stated that work would be kept to a minimum so there would be a lot of time for recreation. He would be able to see his three children whenever he pleased. There would be no court mandates. He added a lake, sun, a tree, birds, a cat, and a cross to represent nature and faith. Bill smiled as he spoke about a place that he could escape to, and where his worries, relationship problems, and financial stressors would be gone.

Tribute mandala

Materials: Drawing paper, markers, oil pastels, and crayons.

Procedure: Clients fill in the mandala with symbols, figures, and/or designs that represent a tribute to someone special in their life. For example, a large heart to represent a mother's love or a trophy for an extraordinary father.

Discussion: Participants share the honor they have bestowed as well as the characteristics of the individual receiving the honor. Examine the significance of the mandala and the impact the admired person/thing has had on the artist's life.

Seasons

Materials: Drawing paper, markers, pastels, and crayons.

Procedure: Clients divide their mandala into four segments representing winter, spring, summer, and fall. Have them symbolize feelings and/or associations to the seasons in each quadrant.

Discussion/goals: Discussion includes sharing of experiences and recollections associated with each season.

Emotions II

Materials: Drawing paper, markers, and oil pastels.

Procedure: Clients create a design using abstract shapes, line, and color to represent various feelings, passions, and sentiments.

Discussion: Participants explore how their emotions affect their behavior. They study their designs for patterns, movement, strength, and feelings evoked.

Figure 36

A 53-year-old male, who had been demonstrating paranoid and delusional thoughts toward his wife, drew a positive mandala. Jack took great care to place the dots in a specific manner, and then he used a ruler to connect the dots with straight lines. He began coloring in the background with a light blue pencil, but stopped after one segment was filled in because "There is still empty space in my life and room for improvement." Jack included SS in his design to represent the first letter of his wife's name and because he liked the way the Ss created her personal logo. Jack carefully added colors to the shapes formed from the dissecting lines, and remarked that the mandala was very colorful. He stated it represented "Adding more color, more fun, in my life." Jack shared his desire to think in a more optimistic manner. He titled the mandala "A Beginning," to represent his work in therapy and the new start he felt he would have in his relationship with his wife. Jack decided to try to be more understanding and less jealous. He promised that he would take their relationship more seriously and try to be considerate and a good listener. Jack included two small triangles of black in his mandala to represent the work he still has to do in therapy to overcome anxiety and fears. When asked, he stated he liked all the colors utilized, but the purple was his favorite because "It is the color of royalty." Jack seemed pleased with his work and left the therapy session with a smile on his face. He appeared to enjoy the positive feedback he received from peers about his work.

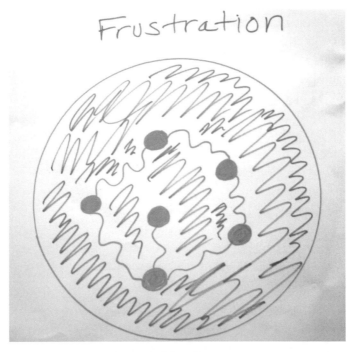

Figure 37

A pretty 36-year-old client named Beth, who was challenged with schizophrenia and delusional thinking, designed this energized mandala. Beth reported a moderate to high stress level as she drew. She had just moved to a new apartment and was feeling anxious, having a lot of difficulty getting used to living by herself and becoming acquainted with the neighborhood. She had previously been living in her mother's house, where she felt safe and protected. Her mother tended to take care of her, doing her errands, cooking, and washing her clothes. In addition, Beth was divorced about one year ago, and she was still upset about leaving her husband, an alcoholic who tended to be verbally abusive and irresponsible.

Beth titled the mandala "Frustration." She stated it represented her entire life. She remarked, "Everything goes wrong, one thing after another." Beth described the orange dots as important people in her life. They include her mother (center dot), sister, daughter (who is being raised by another woman), ex-husband (lowest dot in circle), her therapist (center left), and herself (top dot). Beth connected the dots with wavy lines and remarked they (all the people) add to her anxiety and stress in their own way. The blue scribbles within the mandala represent her constant worry and the tension she feels in her chest and head. She observed that the dots (people in her life) were surrounded by the tension and "they look like they are being carried away by it." Other group members thought her mandala looked like a storm; one woman saw a rush of water, and one man related it to "crazy movement." Beth agreed with everyone and sighed. She stated she enjoyed drawing because it helped her focus on something other than her problems.

Circle of emotion

Materials: Drawing paper, paper plates, markers, crayons, oil pastels, pastels, and drawing paper.

Procedure: Have clients trace a circle. Ask participants to draw an emotion using color and design inside the circle. Then instruct clients to create an environment around the circle. An example of an environment might be a park like setting surrounding a mandala that represents peace and harmony, or a thunderstorm storm surrounding a mandala that symbolizes anger.

Discussion/goals: Discussion focuses on the relationship between the mandala and its background. Goals include focusing, centering, and expression of emotions and feeling.

Energy mandala

Materials: Drawing paper, markers, oil pastels, and crayons.

Procedure: Clients are asked to draw their energy.

Discussion/goals: Clients explore their energy level. Discussion focuses on the way in which the energy is represented (e.g. is it tornado like, strong or weak, perhaps symbolized by small, gently curving lines?). Goals include examining how to best utilize strengths and maintain vigor.

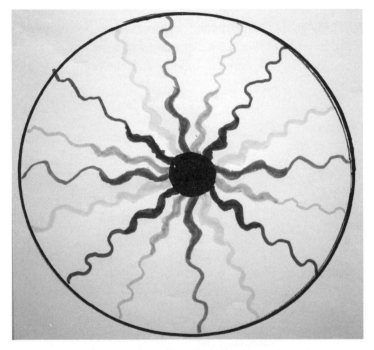

Figure 38

A 49-year-old male named Gary created a black circle to represent the center of his energy. He drew a series of blue, turquoise, green, and yellow undulating lines emanating from the small black circle to represent the strength of his energy. Gary stated that the black center represents his depression, "But it is lifting, so the colored lines are becoming livelier and moving in various ways." The wavy lines represent his improved attitude and willingness to get back out into the world. Gary stated he is ready to think about finding a job, joining clubs or groups, and finding a relationship.

A healing mandala

Materials: Drawing paper, markers, pastels, crayons, and oil pastels.

Procedure: Discuss the idea of healing (e.g. putting an antibiotic and a Band-Aid on a wound helps it heal). Ask group members to create a mandala which helps heal them from past worries and concerns.

Discussion/goals: A discussion centers on the way healing is symbolized in the art work. Clients share strategies to help mend old wounds. Goals include problem solving and exploring coping skills.

Figure 39

Sarah, a woman in her early 50s, designed this colorful healing mandala. Sarah stated she purposely used soft, muted shades to help relax and self-soothe. She chose red, pink, light green, yellow, blue and turquoise. Her lines are soft and mild, "gentle waves." Sarah described the wavy lines as smooth and slow. She liked the pastel-like pink shape and viewed it as calming and healing. Her goal was to create a mandala that lifted her spirits and lessened her anxiety.

Sarah stated she was looking for peace in her life, wanting to divorce an angry, irresponsible man and leave a stressful job. She was looking to find balance and harmony by changing her life style and daily routine and expanding her social life.

Celebration

Materials: Drawing paper, markers, oil pastels, and crayons.

Procedure: Suggest that clients draw a celebration of their life. Have them include positive symbols related to various stages of their life. These symbols may include people/pets, awards, and achievements such as learning to drive or swim. Suggest participants also include where the celebration would take place and what would be occurring.

Discussion/goals: Goals include increase self-esteem and acknowledgement of positive experiences.

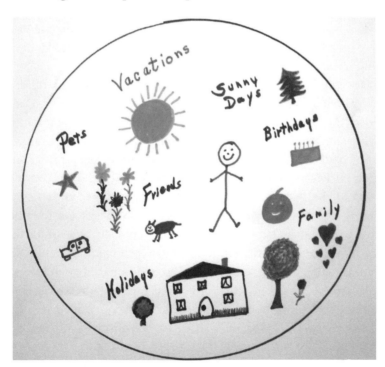

Figure 40

A 27-year-old man named Dan, who recently experienced a near fatal manic episode, included symbols of joyful events and positive feelings in his mandala. He included himself (a stick figure with a cheerful smile leaning a little towards the right of the circle). Dan remarked that he felt well and was ready to continue his studies, go back to college, and resume his life.

Dan had abruptly stopped taking his medication, began smoking marijuana, and quickly spiraled out of control. He ended up in the emergency room for minor injuries sustained during a head-on crash. Dan wasn't aware what was happening or that he nearly killed himself when his car slammed into a tree; luckily he was almost unscathed. He had been smoking pot and drinking large amounts of alcohol. He was escaping from his problems and frequent anxiety attacks that were increasing in intensity. Dan remarked that he was "stupid" and promised he would never behave in such a manner again. He blamed his irresponsible behavior on lack of sleep and school-related stress.

Dan shared that he had a wonderful childhood and a mostly positive college experience. He complained that this past semester was particularly difficult. He "bit off more than he could chew," taking more than 18 credits in one semester.

He reported a supportive family and very pleasant household. He spoke about vacations such as trips to the Jersey shore and Disney World™ in Orlando, Florida. Dan drew his house to represent the warmth and support his parents and siblings provide. He included his pet dog Sam and wrote the word "pets" to represent an array of birds, turtles, mice, cats, frogs, fish, and rabbits he nurtured over the years. He included a pumpkin to symbolize festive Halloween parties and an evergreen tree to symbolize treasured Christmas get-togethers. Flowers, trees, and a large orange sun represent Dan's energy, positive outlook, enjoyment of the outdoors, and appreciation of nature. Dan symbolized his family via the white, traditional style house and brown assorted hearts (left side of mandala). He stated that his family means everything to him; his parents have always helped him cope with adversity. He stated he wanted to "be normal" and make his parents proud once again. His goal was to graduate in two years and become a computer programmer, working for a large company in Silicon Valley, California.

Kaleidoscope[9]

Materials: Drawing paper, markers, crayons, oil pastels, and acrylic paints.

Procedure: Explain what a kaleidoscope is and define it. Show group participants pictures of various designs created in the style of a kaleidoscope. Next suggest that participants create their own kaleidoscope art within the circle.

A kaleidoscope is a circle of mirrors containing loose, colored objects such as beads or pebbles and bits of glass. As the viewer looks into one end, light enters the other end creates a colorful pattern, due to the reflection off the mirrors.

Discussion: Explore the colors, patterns, and shapes. Examine whether the artist sees anything symbolic in his art, such as an image or significant pattern. Discuss the idea of shifting patterns and multiple reflections. Have clients share how these concepts may relate to their life, e.g. change in life style and/or relationships, being able to view situations from many angles, and being able to see people and oneself as complex and ever changing.

Figure 41

A female patient named Danielle, diagnosed with bipolar disorder, drew this colorful kaleidoscope mandala. She wasn't able to relate it to specific feelings, but referred to it as a representation of various life experiences. Danielle shared that she had encountered many challenges and changes in her life, "Some good and some bad." She reported feeling more optimistic and stable during the past week. She was becoming increasingly social and beginning to make friends.

Group members admired Danielle's work. They remarked that her kaleidoscope looked like one of the sample photos given out at the beginning of the session. One woman kept shouting, "Yours is the best one." A young man named Terrence told Danielle how talented and creative she was. Danielle replied, "All of the artwork is good," but she had a slight smile on her face. She obviously enjoyed the attention and the praise. She was able to remember playing with a simple kaleidoscope as a youngster and admiring the beautiful colors and designs formed.

Figure 42

A 28-year-old man named George, who was diagnosed with bipolar disorder, designed this kaleidoscope mandala. He focused on the purple star in the center, which represented him. Everything else emanated from the star. He surrounded himself with a yellow, thinly outlined circle, "for protection." The small gray squares represented some of the people in his life who are there to support him; they included his father, brother, and close friends. The reddish purple circles symbolized group members, and the green triangles were "People I know and say hello to, but am not friends with." George liked the colors and the way the lines intersected with each other. He stated he was trying to make the mandala look like the kaleidoscope images he remembered seeing when he was a child. He related to the symmetry of the design, stating he liked neatness and cleanliness. He was hoping to lead a better balanced life style and to improve his eating and sleep habits and patterns.

Expectations

Materials: Markers, crayons, oil pastels, and colored pencils.

Procedure: Instruct participants to represent their expectations utilizing design, images, and color.

Discussion: Explore each participant's expectations regarding their life, friends, co-workers, neighbors, family members, and themselves. Discuss whether or not their expectations are being met, and if not explore how clients may attain specific goals. Explore whether their hopes are too high, too low, or realistic. Examine if their expectations have changed over the years or have remained about the same.

Black/white mandalas[10]

Materials: Black pastel paper, and white pencil.

Procedure: Create a design within the circle using white pencil on black pastel paper.

First start with black pastel paper (symbolizing the void, unformed spirit, black being all absorbing). Then use a white pencil (symbolizing light, manifest spirit, white reflects all light) to bring forth the inner light, to illuminate the symbol. An empty circle is drawn on the paper, thus being a receptive container for our energies. To receive a symbol, we go into meditation. As we meditate, with the intention of directing transforming light upon a given situation (meditation would consist of listening to soothing music for about 5–7 minutes). The pencils and paper are visualized full of vibrating atoms—energy/light—and we imagine the point of the pencil as our point of focus in the drawing meditation. In the act of drawing, we quickly get feed back when our mind drifts because the drawing becomes dull and flat. Pencils, if not sharp, cause the paper to get waxy and this has a tendency to flatten out the mandala. So, as we work outwardly, we have to work inwardly to stay aligned to the creative source who is really doing the work.

Working with white on black: The exercises are designed to allow the radiance of the mandala to emerge. Therefore, before any color is used, the mandala is illuminated with white.

Not all the black is covered, as the symbol is most powerful when some areas of black are left, giving the white a strong background contrast.

Discussion: Examine the following phrase: "In developing our own symbols, our own sacred art, and bringing them into form to share and help heal the world, we are confronted with creativity, light, intuition, beauty, and love." Discuss the significance of using black and white (contrasts); explore opposites, and all or nothing thinking.

World mandala[11]

Materials: Provide a circular outline of the globe, markers, colored pencils, and oil pastels.

Procedure: Suggest to clients that they that they use shapes, color, lines, and images to represent their view of the world.

Discussion: Explore the way the mandalas were created. Do they represent a positive or critical view of the world? Observe which parts of the mandala are emphasized. Explore the personal world of group members. Examine how their environment, relationships, and work conditions affect them. Discuss the effect that world events have on clients' thoughts, feelings, and behaviors.

Comfort mandala

Materials: Drawing paper, markers, crayons, and oil pastels.

Procedure: Instruct participants to design a mandala that symbolizes *comfort*. Suggest they include people, places, and things that make them feel calm and at ease and/or draw images, shapes, and designs that represent serenity.

Discussion: Explore what comfort means to each individual and how each person portrays it in his mandala. Discuss ways to find peace and tranquility in life such as meditating, listening to guided imagery, taking one day at a time, positive self-talk, and helping others.

Three circle mandala

Materials: Drawing paper, markers, crayons, and oil pastels.

Procedure: Create a mandala out of three concentric circles. In the first circle have participants draw and/or write their greatest inspiration. In the second circle have them draw and/or write their values and beliefs, and in the third circle have them draw and/or write their most important quality or personality characteristic. Instruct clients to surround and fill in the circles with colors and designs that are self-representative.

Discussion: Examine values, beliefs and thoughts about one's strengths and achievements. Self-esteem and self-awareness are focused upon.

Personality mandala

Materials: Magazines, markers, crayons, colored pencils, markers, and oil pastels.

Procedure: Direct participants to use images, shapes, colors, words, and magazine photos to represent various personality characteristics (e.g. a sun to represent a positive personality or lightning to symbolize anger). Suggest clients use color, shape, or size to emphasize their strongest traits.

Discussion: Explore each participant's unique qualities, and support them to assess their self-esteem. Discuss how their traits affect behavior, attitude, relationships, and mood.

Figure 43
Mandala illustrated in the color insert

Gail, a 48-year-old woman, suffering from depression and anxiety due to a recent loss, designed this mandala, which was representative of her character traits. She stated she was very careful to include as many qualities as she could think of so the work would be complete and "tell her story." Gail shared what every color and many of the shapes represented to her. She began with the orange amorphous shape on the upper right hand side of the circle. She mentioned that the orange represented brightness and her hope for a better future. Gail stated she liked rounded shapes because they are "lovely to look at, yielding and comforting." The darker orange color next to it, and the lighter orange adjacent to the darker orange, represent "The lighter side of my life; the fun I have with my husband and children when I am feeling well." The two dark blue shapes (one on the outer rim of the circle and one near the photo of the mother and two children) represented Gail's blue days. "Sometimes I feel like a weight is on my shoulders and I don't want to do anything. I have little or no energy. Getting through the day is most difficult and I feel guilty." The small wiggly pink shape in the center of the orange represents "The child within me. Sometimes I wish I could have someone take care of me and I would not have to think." Next to the dark blue shape, on the rim of the circle, is a rectangle of black, which represented Gail's depression and black moods. A small brown rectangle next to it symbolized the days she's bored, and the purple shape adjacent to the brown represents "The strength I am getting back." Next to the purple form are photos of a cupcake, flowers, and a family. Under these photos are the words "fun and private." Gail stated that she loves cake, flowers, children, and her family. She enjoys having fun and going to parties and picnics in the summer. In response to a question about the word, "private," she emphasized that she's a private person and has difficulty sharing in front of others, especially in groups. Gail mentioned that she feels she will say something stupid and she will not be taken seriously. She was also taught not to tell others her secrets. Next to the family is a light and dark purple, semicircular shape, representing "Gentleness, my soft side." The green thick lines represent her need for perfection; "I like things organized and just right."

Gail appeared pleased with her mandala. She liked that it symbolized most parts of her personality and it enabled her to focus on her strengths, not just perceived weaknesses. She stated she was pleased that much of it was bright; she hoped this was positive sign. When asked which part of the mandala she liked best, Gail stated "the family." She remarked that her family is what keeps her going and what keeps her from even thinking about harming herself. She decided she would keep the mandala and share it with her husband and children.

Figure 44

Vince, a young man in his 20s, challenged with schizoaffective disorder, designed this red, black, and blue mandala. Vince appeared focused, docile, and pleasant, but seemed to be enraged under this façade. His parents were authoritarian and were having difficulty accepting his diagnosis. They wanted him to be outgoing, goal oriented, and as interested in learning as he was in the past. His personality and behavior changed dramatically after his first year of college when he felt "An explosion in my head." That was the turning point; he was never the same after that experience. Vince tried to complete assignments and get to classes on time, but he was unable to focus. He became forgetful and apathetic. He stopped caring about his appearance and his hygiene became poor. He became increasingly confused, tired, and lethargic, often desiring long afternoon naps. He clearly had limitations. Before his illness became apparent Vince's parents saw his future as bright and limitless. They are now still in denial, experiencing much difficulty accepting Vince's problem. His parents bother him incessantly to go back to school and get a job so he could support himself. This has been extremely frustrating for

Vince because he knows at this time in his life it is nearly impossible for him to function on a high level.

Vince was very willing to share his mandala and explain how it represented his personality. He stated the main figure, drawn in red, is a "monster octopus." He described it as growing larger and larger; it wants to break through the circle." The tentacles (on the sides of the body) are reaching out. The body is "electric, like electric currents." One client saw the body as representing lightning or electricity, and Vince agreed. After that observation Vince remarked, "The eyes are searching, they look lopsided." Vince didn't mention the mouth, but in the author's view, the mouth appears angry and aggressive with a focus on the teeth. When asked, Vince replied that the figure is happy. The small face under the monster is crying. Vince stated that the small face represents the way he'd like to be. He remarked the monster is holding him back, and not allowing him to be free. The small blue box next to the face represents him feeling boxed in with no place to go. In the center of the monster's body is a small circle, almost like a navel, but upon closer look, it appears to be a face, with two tiny eyes and the so-called navel being a sad mouth.

Vince appears to be holding in a great deal of anger; he may be about to burst. The author believes his parents are pushing too hard and Vince may crack unless they stop as soon as possible. During Grand Rounds staff members agreed and decided to notify his parents to let them know of this possibility, and to set up a family meeting in the immediate future.

The four elements

Materials: Drawing paper, markers, crayons, and oil pastels.

Procedure: Have participants design a mandala including symbols representing earth, air, fire, and water.

Discussion: A few thousand years ago scientists believed the earth was made of these four elements. Discuss each element and how they may represent parts of one's personality. Possible suggestions include:

- *Fire:* energy, faith and passion

- *Earth:* practical and dependable, stable, rooted

- *Air:* intellect, language, reason, awareness

- *Water:* emotion, love, feeling, caretaker, nurturer.

The elements may be seen as the essentials of life, water to sustain life, earth to grow, wind to carry, and fire to destroy and then re-create.

Figure 45
Mandala illustrated in the color insert

A 51-year-old woman named Helene, who was diagnosed with depression and obsessive compulsive disorder, drew a mandala that included representations of earth, air, fire, and water. Helene wanted to make a clear distinction between each element. She remarked that she liked things neat and orderly. She focused on the fire, which she stated symbolized her anger at her family for not being there when she needed them. She remarked that her parents did not understand, and didn't seem to want to understand her feelings. They thought she was pretending to be depressed so she wouldn't have to go to work and attend to her responsibilities. They kept telling her to "get out of bed and do something," referring to her as lazy. Helene was hoping to get support and empathy from them, but either, "They just don't know how to give it, or they are stingy with their affection." Helene was recently divorced and living with them due to financial problems. She had her own small room in the house and was expected to clean, help with the cooking, and pay a portion of the mortgage.

Helene liked the body of water under the fire because it was "smooth and peaceful." She shared that she'd like to float on a tube in the little lake. She also liked the sky and thought the two clouds were cute. Upon further introspection she stated that she noticed a face in the mandala. Helene laughed and remarked that the clouds looked like two eyes, the fire looked like a moustache, the body of water looked like the mouth, and the earth (soil) appeared to be a beard. Helene pointed out that the shading under the clouds would represent the man's nose. She shared that the mandala looked like her ex-husband. Helene revealed that her ex-husband was an alcoholic who was "way out of control." She stated she loved him, but she had to divorce him for her own safety and sanity. He was very nice when sober but verbally abusive when drunk. He had no interest in AA or in becoming sober. She remarked that she had no choice but to leave him; she had given him many chances to get help and change his unhealthy life style, but he "could care less." Helen decided she would title the mandala "Bill's Gone."

Threads mandala[12]

Materials: Drawing paper, markers, crayons, and oil pastels.

Procedure: Ask clients, "What are the colors of the threads (pieces, parts, and events) that make up your life?" Fill in the circle with your life colors.

- *Red:* anger/danger/problems

- *Pink:* love

- *Yellow:* joy

- *Orange:* anxiety

- *Black:* depression

- *Gray:* gloominess/illness

- *Blue:* peace/serenity

- *Green:* stability

- *Brown:* boredom, "being stuck"

- *Purple:* feeling independent and strong.

Discussion: Explore how the colors relate to meaningful events, achievements, obstacles, and overall life satisfaction. Examine the significance of dominant and less utilized colors.

Clock mandala

Materials: Markers, crayons, oil pastels, and colored pencils.

Procedure: Provide the outline of a clock and have participants fill it in. They may place a time on it or just add images, shapes, and designs to it.

Discussion: Discussion focuses on how group members represent time and how individuals view the importance of time in their lives. Questions such as, "Is time passing quickly or slowly?" may be asked to clarify clients' satisfaction or dissatisfaction with their life. Individuals may be asked how they spend their time, and if they are spending it in a fulfilling and satisfying manner.

A 64-year-old woman named Mimi designed this vibrant clock mandala. Mimi was focused on the passage of time, emphasizing how quickly it goes by. She couldn't believe her 26-year-old son was all grown up and living with his girlfriend in her home. She wished he were five years old again, when life was easier for her and she was in control. Now he was in control, pressuring her to give up her house and taking charge of her finances. He wanted to buy her house for a fraction of the cost and have her rent a small apartment nearby. If this occurred she would be dependent on him for most of her rent, food, shelter, and various other needs. Reluctantly, Mimi was willing to make this sacrifice so her son would like her and stay close. She was fearful, though, that he might not be responsible, and might eventually lose the house, lose her rent money, and leave her homeless.

Figure 46

With extra support and assistance from the author Mimi began working on her mandala. She was encouraged to choose markers, pastels, or crayons, and let the colors and shapes flow. She did just that. Mimi began with the small, black center dot. Surrounding the black dot is a moderately sized spiral that stops at another black dot about halfway through the circle. She was able to relate the dots to herself, starting her life journey at the center of the circle and stopping halfway. She stated she stopped living when her husband died a few years ago. The vivid colors and the movement of the design represent her life as it used to be. In the past she led a rich, full life, full of laughter, fun, and travel. Her husband was very solicitous and carefully planned vacations to lovely resorts a few times a year. They also took day trips to New York City and Philadelphia, dining at exotic restaurants and seeing the newest plays on Broadway. Sunday mornings were relaxing; Mimi's husband made pancakes and eggs while she slept extra late. She remarked she felt like a queen.

Mimi carefully circled each number on the clock. When asked about this emphasis, she remarked that while she drew the circles she was thinking that she wished she could not only stop time, but actually go back in time. During discussion she shared that if given a choice, she would go back 20 years to when her son was four years old, and she and her husband were in their prime. Mimi remarked that people don't appreciate the life they have until it is too late. "The young don't know what they have." The base of the clock is a thin, small turquoise rectangle. Mimi explained that the clock is precariously balanced because it represents the uncertainty of life.

Labyrinth[13]

Materials: Drawing paper, markers, crayons, and colored pencils.

Procedure: Describe what a labyrinth is and define it. Have group members share their interpretation of the meaning of labyrinth. Show examples. Direct participants to design their own unique labyrinth and suggest they try to relate it to their life, current circumstances or an aspect of their existence.

1. A labyrinth is an ancient symbol that relates to wholeness. It combines the imagery of the circle and the spiral into a meandering but purposeful path. The labyrinth represents a journey to our own center and back again out into the world. Labyrinths have long been used as meditation and prayer tools.

2. A labyrinth is a set path that winds to a center and back out again. There is just one path that leads in and out, there is no way to become lost or trapped.

3. A labyrinth differs from a maze. To qualify as a maze, a design must have choices in the pathway.

Discussion: Explore the intricacies of the designs and the path created. Examine if there is a clear pathway or a complex series of curves and lines. Examine how the simplicity or complexity of the configuration relates to one's life, problems, and obstacles to recovery.

Guardian angel

Materials: Drawing paper, markers, oil pastels, and crayons.

Procedure: Instruct participants to create a mandala representing their guardian angel or guardian spirit, their protector.

Discussion: Explore the impact that this spirit has on one's attitude, mood, and behavior. Questions for discussion include:

- Is this special advocate real or imaginary?

- In what ways are you or have you been a guardian angel for someone in your life?

- Share how your guardian angel mandala might reflect strength, courage, security, hope, guidance, serenity, and balance.

- Is it possible that in some ways you are your own guardian angel?

- What feelings did you experience while drawing the mandala and then viewing it?

Notes

1   If a client feels uncomfortable, he may just focus on the male or female side instead of both.

2   www.mandaloodle.com, accessed July 12, 2012.

3   Dream catcher description: http://healing.about.com/cs/native/a/dreamcatcher.htm, accessed July 12, 2012.

4   Modified from www.marycampbell.net/eye.htm, accessed September 17, 2012. It would not be advisable to use this directive with paranoid or most schizophrenic clients. High functioning individuals who are challenged with depression and light to moderate anxiety might derive the most benefit.

5   The cultural and religious associations to the number eight are quoted from Wikipedia and http://www.biblestudy.org/bibleref/meaning-of-numbers-in-bible/8.html, accessed July 12, 2012.

6   This project can also be presented by having clients draw their illness in the center of the circle and use magazine photos to surround it with healing pictures. This method would be especially useful with older adults.

7   Outlined pictures of birds may be found on Google Images™ or other sites on the web, copied and traced onto poster board to be used as templates.

8   The mandalas provide a safe means to express blame and culpability about past mistakes and wrongdoings.

9   Definitions for kaleidoscope: 1. Wikipedia, 2. Bing Dictionary (www.Bing.com), pictures can be found on Google Images.

10 *Drawing Holy Mandalas* by Shauna and Robert Kendall, Modified and shortened to suit client's needs. (Shauna and Robert Kendall are based on the Gold Coast, Australia. They wish to acknowledge that the inspiration for this article comes from the work of Dr. Judith Cornell Ph.D., author of *Mandala: Luminous Symbols for Healing* (1995) Wheaton, IL: Quest Books. See www.Heavenearthhealing.com, accessed July 12, 2012.

According to Raja Yoga and Hindu philosophy, this work of bringing in the light builds up an etheric or astral blueprint of energy in and around the body, which strengthens with each practice. This blueprint will eventually affect the physical body and this is why mandalas or sacred symbols are often used to promote healing.

Carl Jung writes: "When I began drawing the mandalas, I saw that everything, all paths I had been following all the steps I had taken were leading back to a single point—namely, to the midpoint. It became increasingly plain to me that the mandala is the centre. It is the exponent of all paths. It is the path to the centre, to individuation." Jung, C. G. and Jaffé, A. (1965) *Memories, Dreams, Reflections.* New York: Random House.

11 Outline of globe may be obtained from Google Images.

12 The colors and associations used were chosen by author specifically for this particular project.

13 http://www.lessons4living.com/labyrinth.htm. See Google Images for examples of labyrinths, and also Amazeing Art, http://amazeingart.com/media-contact/mazes-labyrinths-faq.html, accessed July 12, 2012.

Chapter 2

Self-Awareness

With our busy schedules, it might be difficult to think about who we are, our strengths and weaknesses, our drives and personalities, our habits and values. Many people just aren't inclined to spend too much time on self-reflection. Even when personal feedback is presented to us, we're not always open to it.

Self-awareness is important for many reasons. It can improve one's judgment and help identify opportunities for personal growth and professional development. Self-awareness builds self-esteem and confidence. It helps individuals decide which direction their life should be following and what their needs and desires are.

Being self-aware includes acknowledging and understanding:

- wishes and desires

- strengths

- weaknesses

- motivation or health and happiness

- challenges

- relationships with others

- barriers to achieving wishes

- belies and values

- self-esteem.

If an individual wants to change his life in any way, he needs to know and understand himself before he can take action. He must be aware of his desires, fears, dreams, goals, and motivations. If he is unhappy or indecisive, he must have a plan and know what has to be completed in order to head in the right direction. Until an individual recognizes his purpose, thinking patterns and life path, he will have difficulty forging ahead and overcoming obstacles.

Inner/outer

Materials: Paper plates, drawing paper, markers, oil pastels, and crayons.

Procedure: On one side of the mandala have clients draw aspects of their personality they usually keep hidden, and on the other side have them draw parts of their personality they feel comfortable presenting to others.

Discussion: Explore feelings and identity. Examine reasons for sharing certain characteristics and keeping other characteristics and behaviors concealed.

Figure 47

Jacob, a 31-year-old man challenged with bipolar disorder, divided his mandala horizontally. The top half of the mandala represents the chaotic thoughts and voices he occasionally hears, especially when stressed. He stated he has difficulty quieting the voices and sometimes they make him feel very frightened and extremely depressed. He mentioned that it is very annoying to hear voices telling him he is doing a bad job and is a horrible person when he is trying to function at work. He remarked that at times he has difficulty calming his thoughts: "It can be exhausting." Jacob shared that sometimes he hears what sounds like electricity. The small, abrupt zigzag lines are representative of these noises. Tiny boxes represent feeling trapped in "my own mind."

The red half of Jacob's mandala (mind) symbolizes the side of his personality he usually shows to others when feeling well. Jacob stated he doesn't usually share that he has an illness, except with close friends. Most people see him as happy go lucky and friendly. "They think I haven't a care in the world and most of my friends and associates believe that I am secure. It's funny," he said, "exactly the opposite is true. My real personality is much more like the first part of the circle, not the second part." The red segment symbolized the person Jacob wanted to be: bright, cheerful, and easygoing. He wanted to be free of the *static* in his life.

Circle of life

Materials: Drawing paper, markers, and oil pastels.

Procedure: Clients are asked to fill in the mandala with symbols that represent their own circle of life. Encourage them to begin with figures representing their earliest memories.

Discussion: Clients share experiences, recollections, and thoughts about their life. The theme of change is examined as group members share life stages and significant events.

My world

Materials: Drawing paper, markers, crayons, and oil pastels.

Procedure: Participants fill in their mandala with symbols, colors, and shapes that represent their present life. Ask them to include who and what is in their world. What does their world look like? Is there movement and activity; is it colorful or drab and empty?

Discussion: Examine attitudes and feelings about the mandala. Discuss whether the world drawn is actually representative of the clients' life. Discuss positive and negatives of one's world and possible changes that might make it more pleasant.

Figure 48
Mandala illustrated in the color insert

A woman in her late 60s, named Victoria, who was challenged with depression and what seemed like a personality disorder, created this mandala of her world. She stated that it showed a lot of craziness and chaos. People weren't included in it because she felt alone, even though she lived with her daughter and son-in-law. Victoria remarked that the mandala was representative of what was going on in her brain. She stated her thoughts were racing, and she wasn't sure where to live or what to do with her life. She was thinking about going back to work and moving to her own apartment. She felt unwanted and cramped in her daughter's house. "They see me and ignore me."

She stated the design symbolized a combination of emotions, which included anger, frustration, uncertainty, and anxiety. Victoria agreed with group members who observed her artwork, "that the mandala was very busy but beautiful."

Victoria shared that she was similar to the mandala because she was always busy "doing nothing." When asked, she remarked the swirls in the background represented going round and round in circles. The leaf-like tails represented trying to find a direction, a goal. The lines symbolized not knowing which way to go. The day she drew this mandala Victoria came to the therapy session very dressed up, as if she was going to work. She said she felt silly, but "was practicing," wanting to see if she could look the way she used to look when she went to work. She would take a lot of care with her hair and make-up, and wear attractive suits. Victoria did enjoy the attention she received while wearing a beautiful red skirt suit. She titled the mandala "Running Scared."

Past, present, future

Materials: Drawing paper, markers, oil pastels, and crayons.

Procedure: Instruct clients to divide their circle into three segments. One segment will be *the past*, one will be *the present*, and the last will be *the future*. Suggest group members fill in the segments with images and symbols that represent their thoughts about these periods of time.

Discussion: Clients share feelings about past and present experiences, and their attitude toward the future. Goals, dreams, memories, achievements, regrets, and obstacles are examined. Explore which segment of the mandala is most positive/negative. Discuss whether the order in which the parts were drawn holds significance.

Figure 49

While designing this mandala, a young woman in her early 20s named Randi focused mostly on the present. Randi drew her house using a light green marker, with flowers, clouds, and birds flying overhead. The house is outlined but not filled in, and it has a door but no windows. Smoke is billowing out of the chimney. Randi stated her house is not a happy one. "My parents are going to get a divorce when I begin college next fall and they are always arguing." She reported that they try "to get her to take sides" and she hates being put in the middle of their struggle. She expressed anger at her father for having had an affair, and annoyance at her mother for "allowing him to get away with it." She shared that her home used to be so pleasant and so much fun: "There used to be a lot of laughter in the house." The word "School" written on top of the figure representing Randi symbolized the past. Next to Randi is "a trampoline" (a rectangular shape with a grid). Randi mentioned she used to love to attend school and play on the trampoline in gym class. She shared that she felt free and joyful. Randi sighed when comparing the past with the present. She stated she knows things will never be the same. She longed for the carefree childhood she so enjoyed. Randi symbolized the future with the word "tomorrow" and a sketch of a cat. She expressed the desire to adopt a cat, hoping that talking care of a pet might help her feel needed and might comfort her. She hoped that when she left her parents' home she would feel calmer. She was afraid that she would never be as close with either of her parents again, but knew she would need to find new friends in the future and additional means of support.

Relapse prevention/recovery

Materials: Drawing paper, markers, oil pastels, and crayons.

Procedure: Participants fill in the circle with symbols of feelings, behaviors, figures, and items that will aid in recovery from addiction, illness, and/or psychological issues such as anxiety and depression.

Discussion: Group members share self-help and coping techniques as illustrated in their mandalas. They explore ways to stay physically and emotionally healthy and avoid future relapses. Participants may use the mandala as an important reminder of ways to remain strong and in control.

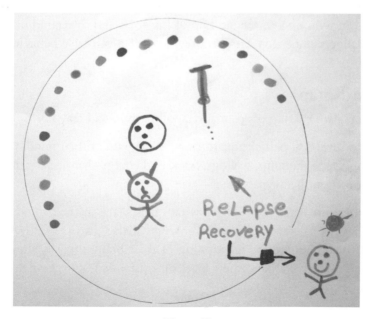

Figure 50

Mark, a 37-year-old male, recovering from addiction to cocaine, barbiturates, and alcohol, drew his thoughts about relapse and recovery. He described his mandala as "eye opening." Mark includes himself, represented by the sad face, the "devil" (situated under the sad face) and the "happy man" (situated outside of the circle). He explained that when he was taking drugs and drinking he turned into a different person. He characterized this person as mean, sometimes violent, irresponsible, and angry (the devil). He stated he was completely out of control. Mark described an instance where he almost killed a man in a fist fight. He couldn't remember what triggered his fury, but his cousin told him it began during an argument about his long-time girlfriend. Ironically, he won the fight but ended up losing his girlfriend because of his reckless behavior and addiction. Mark's physical and psychological health was beginning to deteriorate, and he knew he couldn't continue leading such a self-destructive life. His goal was to stay sober and start a new life. He wanted to find a job, buy a car, rent an apartment, and perhaps marry some day. Mark described the colorful dots that line part of the mandala as positive character traits that would help him accomplish his goals. Mark was able to share a few of these traits, some of which included strength, patience and perseverance. He wanted to take the mandala with him, to remind him of his goals and to remind him of the dangers associated with his previous self-destructive behavior.

Mind map[1]

Materials: Drawing paper, markers, oil pastels, and crayons.

Procedure: Ask participants to create a diagram of their mind. Have them include thoughts, feelings, fears, and energy that occurs around and between their synapses.

Discussion: Participants share what takes place in their mind and the clarity or fuzziness of their thinking. Clients discuss healthy and erroneous thinking, the functioning of their brain, the way they are dealing with issues, and their level of satisfaction with their mood, attitudes, and behavior.

Empowering mandala[2]

Materials: All-purpose paper, any type of paints, markers, water, and brushes.

Procedure: Ask participants to create a mandala that encompasses personal symbols of power and strength. Suggest they think about their positive characteristics and then form images, shapes, symbols, and designs that are representative of their vigor and vitality.

Discussion: Explore how self-confidence and strength is illustrated in the mandalas. Examine unique characteristics, affirmations, and each individual's life force.

The unknown

Materials: Drawing paper, markers, oil pastels, and crayons.

Procedure: Have clients fill in the circle with colors and designs that represent the future.

Discussion: Examine positive and negative thoughts, as well as fears and excitement regarding future experiences. Encourage clients to share feelings evoked by the images created.

Who am I?

Materials: Drawing paper, markers, crayons, and oil pastels.

Procedure: Participants answer this question by symbolizing various aspects of their personality in their mandala. Examples may include hearts to represent a loving person and bright colors to represent a vibrant personality.

Discussion: Discussion focuses on exploring one's interests, personality, and unique characteristics. Explore how self-awareness yields greater self-esteem, identification of wants and needs, and enhancement of the ability to better understand and utilize coping techniques.

Figure 51
Mandala illustrated in the color insert

A woman in her 30s, named Lisa, attempted to answer the question, "Who am I?" through the use of color, shape, and symbolism. Lisa related the mostly vivid colors of the mandala to her desire to "stand out" and be noticed. She remarked that she loved interacting with people and admitted to enjoying center stage. She was a flamboyant dresser, frequently wearing rather outrageous outfits such as bright chartreuse mini skirts, animal print tops, and fishnet stockings with high patent leather boots. She often wore a large floppy hat and gold trimmed sunglasses. Her hair was adorned with purple streaks. Lisa showed off ostentatious tattoos and a variety of piercings, which included her tongue, outer ear lobe, and upper lip. Lisa related the small, yellow semicircle (lower center) to her happy days, and the assorted shades of green to serenity. She viewed the turquoise and blue tints to more thoughtful and introspective moods. The reds and oranges represented her zest and quest for love. Lisa wanted a relationship with a man very badly. She had romantic ideals of a knight in shining armor sweeping her off her feet and saving her from her humdrum life. The areas of black represented her depression and black moods. These were times when Lisa isolated and focused on everything that was wrong with her life and with herself. She would sleep all day and overeat at night; her self-esteem would plummet. Lisa placed the small pink flower on the left hand side of the design to represent beauty. The *eye* or *fish-like* blue teardrop shape on the other side of the circle represented the sadness she still feels periodically. This writer noticed that the design looked like a face (the pink flower and blue teardrop would be the eyes, the pink and orange triangle would be the nose, and the green, orange, and yellow semicircles combine to create the mouth, which would appear down turned). Lisa was asked if she saw anything in her design, and after a few minutes she also saw the face, and then laughed. She remarked that she didn't try to create a face, but "clearly sees it now." Lisa was able to relate it to herself because it was composed of "happy and sad colors, lines, and shapes." Lisa particularly liked the idea of the flower and teardrop designs representing the eyes because she knew there were often times when she felt both sad and happy at the same time, "The flower is the brighter part of me and the fish (teardrop) is the sad part."

Figure 52
Mandala illustrated in the color insert

A 45-year-old woman named Maryellen, suffering from depression and very low self-esteem, drew herself as a teenager. She stated when she was very young she "looked great. All the boys liked me. I had a lot of friends." She considered herself very cool. "I had colorful hair and wore the latest clothes. My skin was smooth and wrinkle free; my eyes were wide and clear. I had a lot of hope and excitement about my life." Then at the age of 21 she married a man who was physically and verbally abusive. He didn't allow her to visit with friends and disliked her family. He was sloppy and insisted she do all of the housework, cooking, and grocery shopping. Maryellen felt more like a servant than a wife. She finally divorced him at age 26, and remarried at age 30, to a man who was challenged with alcoholism and cocaine addiction. He also was verbally abusive, and she eventually left him after ten years of "hardship." She has been single for five years since the divorce. Maryellen shared that it has been difficult meeting people; she had been unsuccessful at internet dating. "Once I met a very unstable man who thought he was king of the world, literally. Another man had difficulty communicating, he whispered." Maryellen was recently laid off from her job as an administrative assistant. She had been working at the insurance company for 15 years. She has been unable to find a job and believes she has been turned down because she's older and overweight. Maryellen stated she wished she could go back in time and "do things differently." One client remarked that each day is a new day, and Maryellen acknowledged that she needs to challenge her negative thinking.

Transitions

Materials: Drawing paper, markers, crayons, colored pencils, and oil pastels.

Procedure: Clients are given the outline of a tree with thick, bare branches emanating from it. They are asked to glue the tree within the circle and fill in the branches with images, words, colors, and shapes that reflect various changes they have experienced, are experiencing, or anticipate in the future.

Discussion: Participants explore feelings, thoughts, behaviors, reactions, and moods associated with change and life transitions.

Life story

Materials: Drawing paper, markers, crayons, and oil pastels, paper plates.

Procedure: Clients are asked to fill in the mandala with their life story. Suggest they include symbols, shapes, items, figures, words, colors, etc. that represent their life from birth to the present.

Discussion: Participants use the mandala as a guide to explain their unique story. Have group members' focus on significant symbols, words, colors, and figures.

Here and now

Materials: Drawing paper, markers, oil pastels, and crayons.

Procedure: Ask clients, "What you are presently experiencing in your life?" Have them describe thoughts, feelings, moods, attitudes, issues, problems, and resulting behaviors. Suggest they fill in the mandala with images related to these descriptions.

Discussion: Encourage participants to explore ways in which the artwork represents their recent challenges and the way they are dealing with both positive and negative aspects of their life.

Portrait

Materials: Drawing paper, markers, pastels, crayons, and paper plate.

Procedure: Clients fill in their mandala with symbols, colors and shapes that are self-representative. The portrait may be realistic or abstract.

Discussion: Clients analyze the symbols drawn and attitude towards their artwork. Explore self-esteem and unique characteristics.

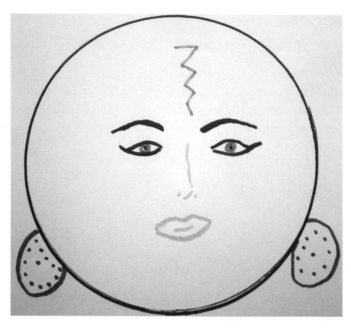

Figure 53

Denise, a woman in her 40s diagnosed with bipolar disorder, drew the face of a woman (herself). The woman has green eyes, a pink nose and mouth, two blue polka dot earrings, and a small green "lightning bolt" down the center of her forehead. She doesn't have any hair. Denise was able to relate to this image in various ways. She shared that the woman doesn't have hair because she is sick and tired of taking care of her own hair, and thought it would be easier not to have any hair at all. Denise was graying and she didn't have enough money to go to a salon to have her hair dyed. She stated she disliked coloring her hair by herself, saying she was very sloppy and messy with the dye. Once she got the dye in her eyes and thought she would never see again. The eyes are green because "my sister has green eyes." She remarked that she has always been jealous of her sister who is "prettier and smarter." The earrings represented her enjoyment of beading and jewelry design, and the lightning bolt symbolized her difficulty concentrating. Denise stated she is unable to focus on reading, which is a great disappointment for her because she used to be an avid reader. She remarked that even skimming through magazines takes too much concentration. She was worried about her ability to remember dates and names. When asked by another group member if she thought the image was pretty, she replied, "Sort of, but she has brain problems."

Figure 54
Mandala illustrated in the color insert

A woman in her 20s named Maris decided to try an abstract, Picasso-like representation of herself. She liked the mandala, but didn't like the way she symbolized her essence. Maris remarked that she made herself appear clown-like and robot-like. She stated that she was trying to show her "softer side," but was unsuccessful at accomplishing this goal. Other group members supported her for trying, but pointed out that most of the lines and angles comprising the picture appeared sharp and controlled. They also wondered about the presentation of the two eyes facing forward. Maris remarked that she was trying to stop being so obsessive and controlling in her life. She was having problems with her fiancé because she always needed to have things done a certain way and admitted to being very unyielding. She stated she couldn't stand it when her boyfriend would leave his dirty socks on the carpet or wouldn't put his dishes in the sink immediately after dinner. She complained that any mess, no matter how small, drove her crazy. Maris related the two eyes facing forward to her desire to copy Picasso, but she also associated them with her inability to be flexible and see things from more than one point of view. While learning about *black and white thinking*, she admitted to being stuck and needing to learn to see the *gray* area. She stated she liked the many bright colors that composed the background, and related the yellow face to feeling brighter and more hopeful.

Name design

Materials: Drawing paper, markers, and oil pastels.

Procedure: The client writes his name in the center of the mandala and draws a design or picture around it, or he creates a design using the letters of his name.

Discussion: Explore how the presentation of each person's name reflects his personality, unique characteristics, and self-esteem. Examine the size of the letters, the colors utilized, and the decorations and figures added to the design. Discuss whether the clients feel positive about keeping their name design within the framework of the circle or would they like to expand outwards? The choice may be related to further discussion about comfort zones, boundaries, and risk taking.

Doorway to the unknown

Materials: Drawing paper, markers, crayons, and oil pastels.

Procedure: Participants draw a door somewhere within the mandala. Suggest that the door may be open, closed, or partly open. Next ask clients to create an environment surrounding the door.

Discussion: Explore the placement, size, shape, and strength of the door, and observe if it is open or closed. Discuss possible meanings of "an open door," versus a "closed door." Connect the sketches of the doors to themes such as being open to change, new ideas, relationships, etc. Explore the saying, "When one door closes, another door opens." Examine the meaning of the environment depicted, and relate it to each individual's feelings about his past, present, and future.

Figure 55

A client named Matt, who was in his late 20s and diagnosed with depression, designed this mandala depicting loneliness. There is a light red window (which he called a door) and a dull gray background. Matt stated he feels lost, like "I'm surrounded by gloom. The window is locked." Matt remarked that he couldn't open the window; he felt there was no way out of his depression. Upon further exploration Matt stated that the window used to be wide open. He liked school, was a good student, and was relatively popular. He had a small circle of friends that he enjoyed "hanging out with." He believed his problems began when his girlfriend of two years ended the relationship abruptly. She emailed him a quick message stating that she met someone new, and would not be seeing him again. Matt was shocked and heartbroken. He was also outraged. She didn't even have the courtesy of telling him this news in person. He lost trust and faith in women. He felt if she could do this to him then who could he trust? This type of thinking and unhealthy generalizations made him believe that nothing was worth doing. "Why try when this type of heartbreak could happen again?"

During discussion the door (window) became a metaphor for being a victim. As long as the door (window) was locked Matt would not recover. He needed to decide to unlock the door (window); he had the power. Matt acknowledged only he could unlock it, but stated he wasn't ready to "go out into the real world; it was too hurtful." Other group members suggested that he take it slowly but keep an open mind. They relayed stories about past broken hearts and how they mended over time. This support seemed to help Matt to some degree. He wasn't ready to open the door, but at least he was gaining the tools, self-awareness, and knowledge to do so in the future.

Hand mandala

Materials: Drawing paper, scissors, markers, etc.

Procedure: Have clients trace their hand in the middle of the circle and then ask them to draw what they see in *the palm of their hand* or what their hand represents about their life and/or personality characteristics. Have them add a background.

Discussion: Explore thoughts about the future, as well as character traits, goals, hopes, and desires.

A woman in her 50s named Molly, diagnosed with clinical depression, drew her hand "crying tears." She stated that her life has been very difficult and she has endured many losses during recent years. A good friend died of breast cancer, another is undergoing chemotherapy now, and another friend moved to a different state last year. She was diagnosed with an autoimmune disease, which left her feeling tired, irritable, and achy. All of a sudden she found herself having to take many medications each day to manage her symptoms, which were "scary and unpredictable." She stated that she was very sensitive to touch and it hurt her if someone even patted her shoulder or arm.

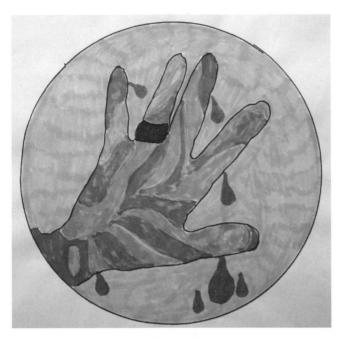

Figure 56
Mandala illustrated in the color insert

Her hand was drawn in green and blue to represent "My hands that hurt and are looking discolored." She related the blue lines to the veins that covered her hands and symbolized "aging." She stated she was seeing and feeling the first signs of arthritis. Her wedding ring is brown because, "I am not happy with my marriage. My husband and I do not get along at all. He is narrow minded and self-centered. He only cares about his work and sports. All he wants to do when he is home is to watch television." Molly remarked that her husband does not empathize with her at all and does little to help her around the house. "He leaves his dirty plates on the table, and clothes on the floor, and "when I complain he says, 'Shut up already,' so I have learned to keep my thoughts to myself. My ring turned from gold to brown and it's sad." A client in the session remarked that Molly's ring appeared tight in the picture. Molly replied, "That's because it is strangling my finger." She explained that the teardrops represented her depression and disappointment with her life. "Every day is so difficult; sometimes I can't even breathe. My anxiety is great." Although Molly says the drops are teardrops, she recently tried to slit her wrists (see the drop by her wrist). The wounds were superficial; she didn't even need stitches, but that was a very loud cry for help. Molly filled in the mandala with a golden yellow background. When asked, she remarked she "has a little hope that she'll feel better since she is in therapy and finds it very helpful." She was interested in learning coping skills to help her manage her feelings and her relationship in a healthier manner. The yellow background also represented her past, which she said was much happier and "pain free."

Life road

Materials: Drawing paper, markers, oil pastels, and crayons.

Procedure: Clients are asked to draw their "life road." Have them include symbols representing various decades of their life, achievements, significant events, obstacles, positive and negative experiences.

Discussion: Explore the significance of the mandalas and the various life events represented. Discuss how clients feel about their life road (are they on track, satisfied or dissatisfied, has the road been smooth, bumpy, or full of major road blocks?).

A 38-year-old man named Carl, challenged with schizophrenia, designed this rather bleak life road. Carl didn't want to say too much about his mandala, but with gentle prompting he answered a few questions posed by the author and group members. Carl stated that the beginning of the road is where the question mark-like shape begins (the claw-like shape). He remarked that he doesn't remember his early years except that he was teased unmercifully in school and stayed mainly by himself. His brothers also teased him and made fun of his inability to get along with others. Carl's brothers played practical jokes on him, which left him angry and frustrated; he could not fight back physically or emotionally. He mentioned that once his brothers wrote vulgar words with marker on the kitchen wall and blamed him; his parents believed his brothers and he was punished severely. Voices telling him he was stupid and bad began plaguing him in his later teenage years. He found them terrifying and his family didn't understand what was happening to him, so

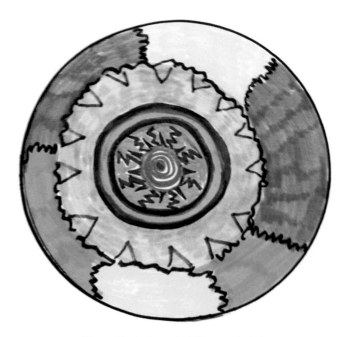

Figure 7: Active mind/images (p.25)

Figure 14: Forgiveness (p.37)

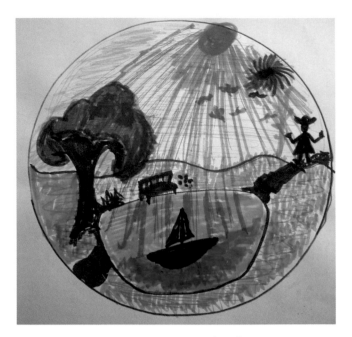

Figure 15: Fantasy (p.39)

Figure 16: Fantasy (p.40)

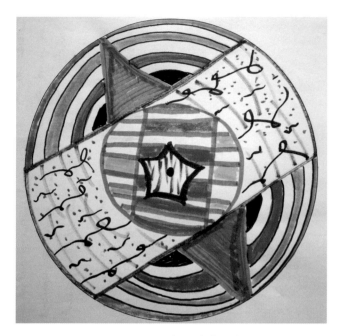

Figure 18: The web (p.44)

Figure 21: Patterns (p.49)

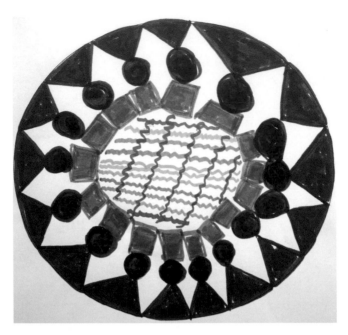

Figure 22: In control / out of control (p.52)

Figure 29: Passion mandala (p.65)

Figure 30: Love mandala (p.68)

Figure 43: Personality mandala (p.98)

Figure 54: Portrait (p.123)

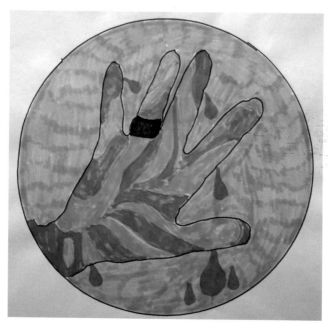

Figure 56: Hand mandala (p.127)

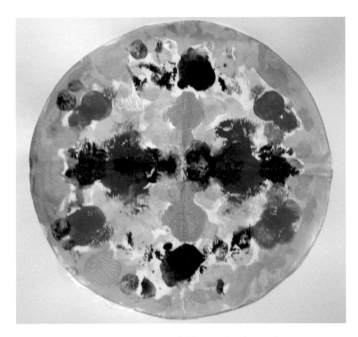

Figure 61: Paper folding print (p.163)

Figure 62: Day dream (p.167)

Figure 63: Mixed media collage (p.172)

Figure 64: Cut shapes (p.174)

Figure 66: Cut shapes (p.176)

Figure 67: Movie poster mandala (p.177)

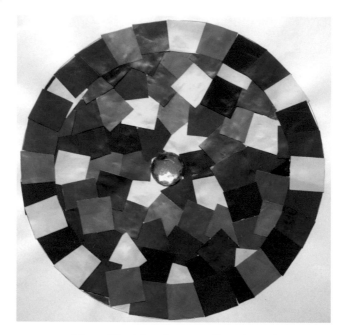

Figure 72: Colored paper collage (p.190)

Figure 73: States (p.196)

Figure 74: Arrow collage candala (p.197)

Figure 75: Mandala mural II (p.200)

Figure 90: Crystals and mandala (p.255)

Figure 96: Mandala inspired poetry (p.266)

they dismissed his complaints as attention seeking behaviors. In high school he continued to be an outcast, but managed to graduate with good grades in science and history. He began to write and found an outlet and some solace in creative writing and journaling. The voices didn't bother him so much when he was engaged in creative endeavors. The thick, black, wavy line in the center of the mandala illustrates the darkness Carl had endured and continues to deal with every day. Every day is a struggle for him, and even with medication and therapy the voices are almost always active. Carl remarked that, "The line doesn't end and it doesn't change shape; it just goes on and on in the same way." When asked if he would ever consider adding color to a future mandala of this sort, Carl stated, "No."

Figure 57

Pie chart

Materials: Drawing paper, markers, pencils, paper plate to trace a circle, and a ruler.

Procedure: Clients trace a circle from the paper plate. Then they use a ruler to divide the circle into three or four segments. The parts of the circle are labeled morning, afternoon, evening, and nighttime. Clients draw what they do during each of these times; they may add a written description if need be.

Discussion/goals: Discussion focuses on how clients spend their work and leisure time, and how they feel during different parts of the day, e.g. it is common for depressed individuals to feel poorly in the morning but become brighter and more energized during the evening hours. Goals include problem solving, self-awareness, and exploring leisure time activities.

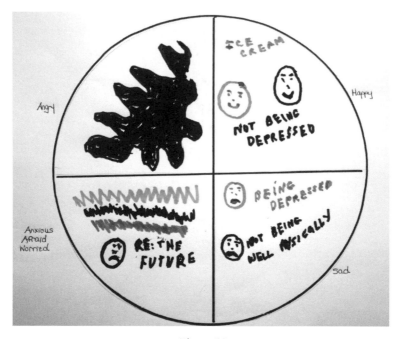

Figure 58

A 29-year-old client named Antoine, challenged with bipolar disorder, chose to divide the mandala into the feelings he experiences during the different parts of the day. The first segment, the morning, shows how angry he usually feels. Antoine remarked that he wakes up very irritable, "Like a black cloud is hanging over my head." He mentioned that he hates to hear the loud alarm buzz and he hates when his mother calls him downstairs for breakfast. "What she really wants is to see if I am dressed for program; she doesn't trust me." He mentioned that his fury feels like a stabbing pain in his chest. Antoine stated that the anger begins to dissipate about 10:00am when he usually has something sweet to eat, like a Snicker's bar.

The second segment represents Antoine's favorite time of day, lunch time, about 12:30 pm. Antoine mentioned that he has chocolate ice-cream almost every day and this special dessert raises his spirits. He usually sees his friend Amelio after lunch and they "hang around" and enjoy each others company. Antoine shared that Amelio is the only one who understands what he's experiencing because he also has bipolar disorder and has been working on addiction issues.

The third segment represents the time period from about 6:00 pm to 9:00 pm. Antoine mentioned he usually feels anxious and confused during that time. This is because he is often alone and watching television, "This is when my mind starts to wander and I think of all the bad things that can happen." He states that he thinks about death and illness. He fears becoming out of control and having to be institutionalized.

Antoine also expresses stress in the last segment of the mandala, which is the nighttime. He reported much anxiety because of poor sleep and nightmares. The nightmares are terrifying, so he wants to stay awake all night to avoid them. Staying awake contributes to depression because Antoine feels exhausted and frustrated. He is currently trying self-hypnosis to help alleviate and/or lessen the nightmares. It was also recommended that Antoine use art therapy to help control the nightmares by drawing them and analyzing them. In this way he would gain control over them and they would not be so internalized.

When Antoine viewed his mandala as a whole he was not pleased. He felt that according to what he drew, he is more anxious and depressed than happy. With support and guidance he decided to try to engage in positive activities and relaxation exercises in the evening to help boost his mood. He was not sure which leisure activities he would like to engage in, but he was willing to listen to relaxation CDs and to begin experimenting with watercolors.

Individuality

Materials: Drawing paper, paper plates, markers, crayons, and oil pastels.

Procedure: Clients fill in the circle with unique aspects of their personality.

Discussion: Discussion focuses on moods and feelings. Explore the complexity of group members' thoughts and behavior.

Grid mandala

Materials: Drawing paper, markers, oil pastels, and crayons.

Procedure: Have clients draw, or have pre-drawn circular grids distributed to clients. They will be composed of many evenly spaced, small squares. Next ask clients to fill the squares in with colors and shapes that reflect various moods.

Discussion: Participants reflect on behavioral patterns and moods. Have them explore how the colors and designs reflect temperament during different times of day and in response to various situations.

Wisdom

Materials: Drawing paper, markers, oil pastels, markers, and paper plates.

Procedure: Instruct group members to share their personal definition of wisdom. Next suggest they fill in the circle with figures, scenes, shapes, colors, and items that represent wisdom or times they used good judgment and showed insight.

Discussion: Participants share the ways in which their mandalas represent their astuteness. Explore how people gain wisdom over the years. Examine how having both positive and negative experiences can be beneficial and enlightening.

Managing illness

Materials: Drawing paper, markers, oil pastels, and crayons.

Procedure: Clients are asked to creatively represent a physical and/or psychological illness within the circle, taking up no more than half the circle. Next suggest they create a containment surrounding the illness.

Discussion: Explore the specific illness represented, and the size, shape, and strength of the containment. Have clients observe the width and power of the lines, colors and forms utilized. Examine whether the illness is well controlled or out of control. Discuss how long the illness has been a problem and how long the containment has been surrounding the illness. Examine coping techniques.

Medication mandala

Materials: Drawing paper, old magazines, glue sticks, scissors, and markers.

Procedure: Suggest that clients find images of people taking medication, and glue the photos within the circle to create a collage. Words, phrases, and medicine bottles may also be used. Clients may add colors, shapes, images, words, and phrases representing their feelings about taking medication.

Discussion: Group members share reactions to their mandalas and discuss feelings about taking their medications. The importance of taking medications in a timely and organized manner is emphasized. This directive affords participants the opportunity to share pleasant and unpleasant experiences while taking medications: symptoms, side effects, and health benefits.

Counting blessings

Materials: Drawing paper, pastels, crayons, and markers.

Procedure: Ask clients how often they focus on the pleasures in life instead of the problems and frustrations. Instruct clients to think about what is positive in their life and then they suggest they draw their blessings within the mandala.

Discussion/goals: Examine the way in which group members chose to express their blessings and discuss how emphasizing one's blessings can help individuals cope with depression, problems, and concerns. Explore how blessings often represent achievements in life such as children, a lovely home, good physical health, etc. The artwork provides patients with tangible pictures to observe and examine, and refer back to quickly and easily when needed for extra support and comfort. Goals include increased self-esteem and self-awareness.

Yesterday, today, tomorrow

Materials: Drawing paper, markers, crayons, pastels.

Procedure: Read and discuss the following:

> Yesterday is history,
> Tomorrow is a mystery.
> Today is a gift,
> That's why they call it the present.

Instruct clients to divide their mandalas into three equal parts that will include: *Yesterday* (their past), *Today* (their gift), *Tomorrow* (the future – mystery). Have them symbolize each segment of their life within the mandala.

Discussion: Discussion focuses on the past, present, and future. Examine ways in which various life experiences and expectations affect mood, attitudes, and behavior. Discuss the importance of being mindful.

View of the world

Materials: Drawing paper, markers, crayons, and pastels.

Procedure: Ask group members to fill it in with pictures, figures, and symbols that represent their view of the world.

Discussion/goals: Discussion focuses on the client's thoughts, attitudes, values, outlook, and mood. Explore how group members view the world: Is it a happy place, do they need to protect themselves from it? Do they trust others? Do they see the world as dangerous or helpful and supportive? Examine ways in which they could improve their own world (community, home life, work place) and their environment. Discuss how one's view of the world affects one's attitude toward therapy and working towards health and recovery.

Magical moment mandala

Materials: Drawing paper, oil pastels, markers, and crayons.

Procedure: Suggest that participants fill their mandala with magical moments such as a wedding, graduation, the birth of a baby, etc.

Discussion: Explore extraordinary life experiences and associated feelings by examining the symbols, shapes, lines, and designs that comprise the mandala.

Personal logo

Materials: Drawing paper, markers, oil pastels, and crayons.

Procedure: Discuss various signs and symbols that represent people, places, and things. Share the impact they have on our thoughts, feelings, and emotions. Give examples of symbols, such as a lion represents courage and a dove peace. A shamrock represents good luck and a heart represents love. When we see the Gucci or Tiffany label we know the item is of high quality. Suggest that clients create a logo or symbol within the mandala that represents their special qualities.

Discussion: Explore group members' unique characteristics and messages they verbally and non verbally convey to others about themselves. Examine self-esteem as represented by the specific logos and their placement within the mandala. Discuss features such as the size, color, detail, and relatedness of the logo to the artist. Is the logo positive or negative; is it unusual or a common symbol? Is the individual pleased with it or desiring of something more optimistic and stronger in design and meaning?

The unknown

Materials: Drawing paper, markers, and oil pastels.

Procedure: Have group members participate in a few deep breathing exercises, such as breathing in through their nose for a count of three and breathing out through their mouth for a count of four, and then ask them to imagine themselves walking through a dark, wooded area. Ask participants to think about how they are feeling, and what they are seeing, touching, hearing, and experiencing. Suggest they outline a circle using a paper plate and divide their circle in half. Instruct them to draw what is behind them on one half of the mandala and what is in front of them on the other half of the mandala.

Discussion: Discussion focuses on the figures/symbols drawn. For example, did the individual draw a bear behind him or a pot of gold in front to him? Clients may be encouraged to relate what they sketched behind them to their past and what they sketched in front of them to their future. Discussion may include how clients have handled previous situations, are handling their present situation, and thoughts about the future.

Images

Materials: Drawing paper, markers, oil pastels, and colored pencils.

Procedure: Suggest clients fill in the circle with images that flow through their mind during the course of the day.

Discussion: Participants share their associations to the images that compose the mandala. Explore how the pictures and symbols work together to create a design. Discuss the significance and intensity of the thoughts. Questions such as "Does the imagery motivate you to take action?" and "Is the imagery positive or negative?" may be examined. Ask clients how their representations are symbolic of their behavior, thoughts and feelings.

Figure 59

A 62- year- old male named Dirk, who was recently diagnosed with bipolar disorder, created a mandala of layers. The first layer represented his "calm side." He shared that he feels peaceful on sunny days when he is walking in the park or fishing with his buddies. He remarked that he doesn't stay calm for long. The next layer represented chaotic thoughts and anxiety. Dirk mentioned that his moods change rapidly and he had the capacity to be calm one minute and highly stressed the next minute. "When I am anxious, all I see and hear becomes blurry. I think in circles and nothing makes sense." The clouds and birds represent "coming out of the chaos" and the shape situated on the upper right side of the paper represents "a dark yellow, hot sun."

Dirk stated the sun prevents him from darkness (depression). He associated the sun with his family, particularly his wife and children. "My wife looks after me although she can be annoying sometimes. She can be bossy, making sure I take my medicine and don't sleep too late in the morning. I know, though, that she does this because she loves me and wants me to be well."

Notes

1   A synapse is a connection, which allows for the transmission of nerve impulses.

2   Life force may be characterized as the flow of life-giving energy. Our decisions and behaviors help cultivate our life force.

Chapter 3

Painting

Mandala painting allows for spontaneity and freedom. It is a medium that gives clients the ability to experiment with color, style, and movement. Paint is particularly useful for clients who need to break free from rigidity and structure. It allows for flexibility and flow in artwork.

Watercolors may be easier to work with for some clients. Clients maintain artistic control because they determine how dark or light, thin or thick the paint will be by adding more or less water to the mixture. It is a type of paint that is generally not too messy, easier to clean up, and can be painted over a pre-drawn outline. The watercolors that come in cases are contained and straightforward to manipulate.

Acrylics take a little more skill, but the colors can more easily be blended and mixed to form new shades. Individuals may use these paints to create abstracts or their own creative designs. They are easier to use and quicker to dry than oil paints.

There are paints that come in thick marker-like pens that can be dabbed onto the paper. These are very non-threatening, fun and simple. They can be used to create a variety of designs including dot abstracts. Finger paints can be used for clients who are ready to express themselves freely. Creating a mandala while finger painting to music can be an enjoyable exercise for clients who are ready to be messy "for art's sake." It is a pleasurable and imaginative exercise that allows the client to express himself freely and affords him the opportunity to change his mind as many times as he pleases. Other painting techniques include sponge painting, painting with a mini roller, painting by blowing through a straw, marble painting, and using a brush to flick the paint on the paper like Jackson Pollock (to be worked on in a very structured environment with high functioning clients).

I suggest using non-toxic and washable paints; clients can become upset if their clothes become dirty or if they have difficulty cleaning their hands. As with other mediums, it is important to determine if the population you are working with will benefit from and be focused enough to engage in this medium. Mandala painting allows for greater control and less chaos since there is a structure provided.

Sponge painting[1]

Materials: A variety of sponges cut into shapes, poster paint, small bowls, and paper.

Procedure: Pour the paint into the bowls. Instruct clients to dip the sponges into the paint and press the sponges on the paper. Encourage them to create a design within the circle.

Discussion/goals: Discussion focuses on the artwork and its symbolism. Goals include enhancing abstract thinking, creativity, focusing, and spontaneity.

Impressionism[2]

Materials: Watercolors, water, and brushes.

Procedure: Briefly introduce the style of the impressionists and show sample paintings such as those of Monet and Manet.

"Often Impressionism, a theory or style of painting originating and developed in France during the 1870s, was characterized by concentration on the immediate visual impression produced by a scene.

The French painters depicted the natural appearances of objects by using dabs or strokes of primary unmixed colors in order to stimulate actual reflected light.

The style was called impressionism because the artists were not as exacting about painting a realistic picture. They used many short brush strokes, applying paint thickly, to create the idea, or impression, of a subject."

After introducing the style ask participants to paint a mandala using this technique. Suggest that clients use their senses and focus on how they are feeling at the moment.

Discussion: Explore how the mandala reflects feeling and emotion. Observe the colors, movement, images, and shapes. Explore reactions to the method used to paint the mandalas (e.g. sketchy brush strokes, various shades of the paints, and asymmetrical compositions). Have clients relate the ethereal or spontaneous quality of their work to thoughts about their own personality style and way of handling relationships and daily life.

Mindful painting

Materials: Acrylics, watercolors or tempera paints, brushes, pencils, and paper.

Procedure: Suggest that clients experience the paint by brushing it within the mandala without thought to design or quality of the artwork. Support the clients to focus on the feeling of the brush and paint on the paper. Support them to become one with the brush. Have participants observe the paint strokes, colors, and shapes created.

Discussion: Discussion focuses on how well the group members were able to observe the experience, feel the movement, and refrain from judgment. Goals include stress reduction, being in the moment, and creative expression.

Fabric or tee shirt mandala[3]

Materials: Fabric markers, fabric paint, cardboard, and white tee shirt or large piece of white cloth.

Procedure: Instruct participants to place the cardboard under the shirt or cloth so the color does not seep through. Have them outline a circle on the tee shirt or cloth with a black permanent marker using a paper plate as the template. Next suggest they use the fabric paint or markers to fill in the circle with symbols, figures, and lines that characterize their personality.

Discussion: Explore the ways in which the symbols and colors are self-representative. Examine the empowerment associated with wearing the mandala as an article of clothing.

Monochromatic mandala

Materials: Acrylic paints, brushes, water, and painting paper.

Procedure: Suggest that participants fill in the mandala using one color that best represents their present mood. Have them add various forms, lines, patterns, and textures to further symbolize their feelings. Ask clients to rate their mood before and after creating the mandala.

Discussion:

1. Clients share the meaning of the colors and shapes.

2. They explore whether or not their mood changed while working on the mandala.

3. Participants examine reasons they feel the way they do (e.g. low or high self-esteem, relationship issues, stress, etc.).

4. Explore if clients experience changes in mood throughout the day or week.

5. Have group members share thoughts about utilizing one color (did they feel comfortable using one color, or was it too restricting?, etc.).

Spiral mandala II[4]

Materials: Drawing paper, markers, oil pastels, crayons, and colored pencils.

Procedure: Share the following descriptions and directions written by Yolanda Brand.

> The spiral was the earliest known decoration used in art. The directional flow of the spiral symbolizes our movement through the experiences of life, death, and rebirth. The ancient Celts believed

in this idea and as a result, their myths and legends refer to this journey.

In most cultures, it is a symbol of eternal life. The symbol spirals out infinitely, thus reinforcing the concept of life, death, and rebirth. The whorls represent the continuous creation and destruction of the universe. In terms of rebirth and growth, the spiral symbol can represent awareness of self, beginning at the core or center, and expanding outwardly, as it develops.

It is also a symbol of initiation and the ritual journey through a labyrinth to the sacred realms beyond the center. The center represents complete balance. It is the place where Heaven and Earth merge. Some believe that there is significance to the direction of the spirals. A clockwise spiral symbolizes the sun and represents growth, expansion, and positive cosmic energy. To move sun wise is to be in harmony with the earth. The traditional Gaelic blessing, a'deasail, means good-luck and refers to this idea. The opposite directed spiral, or anti-sun wise motion is used in making geis or spells. This can be confusing since spirals flow both inwards and outwards.

In Celtic art and symbolism, we can intuit a few meanings from the forcefully present spiral:

- evolution and holistic growth

- letting go, surrender, release

- awareness of the one within the context of the whole

- connectivity and union with deific and cosmic energies

- revolutions of time, stars, planets and the way of natural progress.

In terms of spirituality, the spiral symbol can represent the path leading from outer consciousness (materialism, external awareness, ego, outward perception) to the inner soul (enlightenment, unseen essence, nirvana, cosmic awareness). Movements between the inner (intuitive, intangible) world and the outer (matter, manifested) world are mapped by the spiraling of archetypal rings; marking the evolution of humankind on both an individual and collective scale. Moreover, in terms of rebirth or growth, the spiral symbol can represent the consciousness of nature beginning from the core or center and thus expanding outwardly. This is the way of all things, as recognized by most mystics.

Paint your own spirals. Draw spirals. Make spiral symbol mosaics. Use any media that appeals to you to create spirals, and as you do, imagine the controls of your mind loosening with each outward wave created as you move out in a spiral motion of your creation.

This exercise is similar to coloring mandalas. The idea is to get lost in the grandeur of creating. The mandala or spiral symbol is a partner in creation and can launch our dreaming mind into profound realms of awareness.

Discussion: Clients share the symbolism related to the size, movement, and colors of the spirals. Examine how the spirals may relate to one's "inner world" and the idea of growth and expansion.

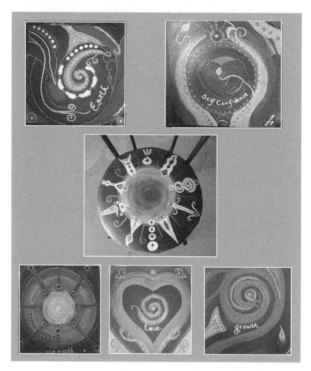

Figure 60
[This lovely mandala was designed by artist Yolanda Brand]

Abstract mandala

Materials: Brayer (small roller), acrylic paints, and painting paper.

Procedure: Use a plastic cutting board or paper plate to spread out the acrylic paint. (Use acrylics that come in tubes.) Squeeze a small amount of the paint on the plate and roll the brayer back and forth over the paint and then roll the brayer within the circle to begin to create a design. Then choose another color and roll it at least partly over the first color. Keep doing this with various colors until a pleasing design is formed. Clients may use whatever colors they please. Suggestion: a mixture of turquoise, mint green, yellow, and pink look well together.

Discussion: Explore the texture, colors, and composition of the mandala. Discuss feelings evoked by the artwork and the creative experience. Share reactions to rolling the paint instead of using the traditional brush.

Finger paint mandala[5]

Materials: Finger paints, paper, a variety of music which elicit different moods (e.g. the big bands, classical, soft rock, rock and roll, jazz), pencils and writing paper, and paper plate.

Procedure: Have clients outline one circle on three different sheets of paper. They will use one sheet for each song. Play a lively tune and have clients begin finger painting. Encourage them to stand up and move to the melody while painting if they are comfortable doing so. After the first song is over suggest that clients write their response to the music, and their thoughts about their design. Follow this procedure for three songs and then as a group discuss the artwork, music, and written thoughts. (The first song may be lively, the second song somber and the third selection calming.)

Discussion/goals: Goals include: expression of various emotions, socialization, expression of thoughts and concerns, and release of tension and energy.

I have used this technique a number of times with depressed clients. Although reluctant at first, they quickly relax and participate fully in the project. Clients frequently state they remember childhood situations and school events while painting. Many individuals are surprised at the memories elicited during this group.

This project can be geared toward many populations. Allowing clients to listen to music such as Beethoven and Bach, and having them write their feelings between songs, helps clients view the project as an art experience that adults as well as children may enjoy.

Swirls and movement[6]

Materials: Watercolors or acrylics, watercolor paper or all-purpose drawing paper, brushes, and water.

Procedure: Ask clients to paint swirls within the mandala using a variety of colors and utilizing a range of brushes. Have them add background color(s) if desired.

Discussion: Examine the movement of the mandala and the way in which the swirls add a playful quality to it. Discuss each participant's "mandala flow" and relate it to each individual's flow of life.

Paper folding print

Materials: Drawing paper, acrylic paints, and scissors.

Procedure: Distribute a pre-cut circle to each client. Have clients fold their circle evenly in half (vertically). Now clients open the circle and add a dollop of paint to each side. Next they close the circle and smooth it down. Have them open it again and they will see an unusual design. Clients now fold their circle downwards (horizontally) and they follow the same procedure using a different color paint. They keep folding the circle in different ways and adding more paint colors until they are pleased with their unique design. They may add more color with a brush to create an even more colorful mandala.

Discussion: Clients share thoughts about the creative process, and examine the colors, shapes, and figures that compose the abstractions. Encourage participants to see if they could relate the mandala or parts of it to personality characteristics, people, or aspects of their life and relationships.

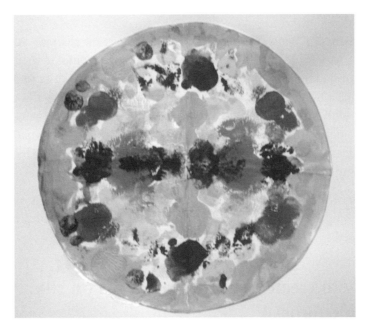

Figure 61
Mandala illustrated in the color insert

A 27-year-old man named Hal, who was challenged with schizophrenia, had fun creating this richly colored design. Hal enjoyed watching the design evolve as he kept adding paint and folding the paper. Hal was pleased because it took minimal skill and effort to create an attractive, complete piece of art. Hal was able to experiment with shape, color, and design. His self-esteem was increased as it became increasingly clear that the mandala would turn out to be an attractive, lively, multihued piece of work. When asked, Hal shared that the mandala looked like a flower. It reminded him of the garden he helped his mother take care of when he was a little boy. He stated that he liked watching the plants and flowers grow and bloom. He remembered eating delicious, juicy tomatoes that were grown in his own backyard. When asked to title the mandala, he called it "Working in the Garden."

Day dream

Materials: Paint, brushes, markers, painting/drawing paper, and paper plates.

Procedure: Clients are given a brief demonstration about mixing colors, specifically making colors lighter by adding white to them, for example: adding white to red to make pink or adding white to green to make a light, mint green. Next participants are asked to fill in the circle with light colors. When the circles are dry suggest that clients fill them in with symbols, shapes and figures that represent what they daydream about during the course of the day. Examples may include thinking about finding a lot of money or getting married.

Discussion: Participants share the reveries, fantasies, and symbols that compose their mandalas. Expectations, hopes, and dreams are explored.

How to create your own mandala on silk: A simple tutorial[7]

Materials:

- a piece of silk in the size of your choice

- a plain wooden frame (cut up a length of wood from a home goods/hardware store such as Home Depot, and nail together)

- pins or hooks to affix the silk to the frame

- two or three watercolor brushes

- three tubs of silk paint (ensure you have pain for iron fixing, and not dyes): red, yellow, and blue—the 1.75 oz (50g) are fine to start with but the larger tubs are more cost-effective

- jar of water

- a tube of water-based resist (liner) to draw lines with— colored or clear

- magic fabric marker (that will disappear within a day or two)

- pair of compasses to draw circles with

- little tubs to mix colors in.

I'm now going to guide you through the process of creating your own mandala, step by step. If you buy a meter (3 feet) of silk at a craft store, fold it in half, make a tiny cut at the edge and then take a good firm hold of the silk and rip it in two. You can do the same again to half the piece once more.

Give your silk a good rinse in water before starting to ensure you remove all substances that might inhibit the flow of the paint.

Pin your silk to the wooden frame, starting with the four corners. Don't be afraid to stretch the silk as it is very tensile. Next, place pins halfway along each edge, always doing the two opposite sides before moving on. This keeps the tension right. Next place the pins half way between each of the pins already in the silk, and so on until it is firmly in place.

Mark the center point of your silk and then draw a few concentric circles with your magic marker and compasses, placing a couple of books underneath to give a proper hold.

Starting from the inner point, draw motifs in each circle with the tube of water-based liner. Complete each circle before you move onto the next one. This is a bit like cake-icing. Make sure the liner penetrates the silk properly and creates a solid line for each shape you draw. Check by holding up the silk to the light to see if there are any gaps. If there are, fill them in. You might want to practice doing this on a scrap piece of silk to get the pressure right. Not too hard so that you scratch against the silk and might bloop large puddles of liner. And also not too light so that the line is too thin and doesn't penetrate the fabric properly.

You might want to look in books or in nature for some ideas of shapes you could include. I love to paint leaves in all shapes and sizes. Remember that the designs don't need to look realistic. Just have fun with this.

Work until you have reached the outer circle and have completed each ring. Allow this resist to properly dry before going on. I normally leave mine overnight or at least from morning until late afternoon. You can speed things up by using the hairdryer.

When the pattern is dry, you are ready to start painting. Please ensure you have the paints and not the dyes, which need to be steam fixed. Pour some of each color into a small tub and "just play around," mixing some colors that you would like to experiment with. Try them out on a piece of kitchen roll to see if you like them. Dilute them as much as you like using water, or simply use them straight from the tub.

Begin painting your mandala from the center outwards. When you apply the paints with the brush, you will find that the color flows until it reaches the lines you painted earlier. So you can now see why it was important to have closed lines if you are painting a leaf and you only want the color to stay within the lines. Just enjoy the process and intuitively go with whatever colors speak to you. Remember, leaves can be pink and turquoise—just allow your creativity completely free flow.

When you come to paint the background, this is a larger area, and when you stop in-between, the paint can begin to dry and form harder edges. If you want to keep a smooth flowing area, try wetting the whole background gently with a larger brush. This will mean that the colors are lighter as the water will dilute them a bit, but the flow will be better. You can also try adding further colors to this larger area and allow them to flow into each other for a more complex look.

When your mandala is complete, leave it drying flat away from the direct sunlight.

You can then unpin your silk artwork and lay it on the ironing board to fix your colors. Don't use a steam setting for this as water droplets can escape and spoil your silk. I recommend using a hot iron and placing a cotton tea towel over your silk. Iron each part for 3 minutes, keeping the iron moving as you go.

If you have used color resist for the pattern, your silk artwork is now complete as the colored lines stay in as part of the design. If you used clear resist, you can now put the silk painting into warm water and gently rinse out the lines. The white silk will show through where the resist was. Roll your silk up in a towel, dab dry and iron as before.

Your beautiful work is now ready to be mounted or used for whatever you choose.

Discussion: Clients share thoughts about the intricate process and the steps involved. Support each client's perseverance, demonstrated by following directions and seeing the project through to completion.

Discuss how the colors and designs are unique, and the way in which they are self-reflective.

Figure 62
Mandala illustrated in the color insert
[This striking mandala was designed by Fiona Stolz]

"Jackson Pollock" drip[8]

Materials: Acrylics, brushes, sticks, sponge brushes with handles, water, and watercolor paper.

Procedure: Explain that Jackson Pollock was an innovative artist who was not concerned with specific images or composition. Pollock was indifferent to positive or negative space. He was known for his "pouring or drip technique." The term "action painting" was used to characterize his unique style. Pollock was able to "view and observe his painting from all directions." His art was immediate; he often used his entire body to form his creations. Pollock was influenced partly by Indian sand painting in the 1940s and work by Mexican muralists and Surrealist automatism.

After this brief description suggest that clients try to work in a similar manner, but on a much smaller canvas. After a circle is outlined on the paper instruct clients to place paint in small cups and either gently pour different colors onto the circle or use a brush to gently flick the paint until a pleasing image is formed. Clients may use the brushes or a stick to further define their work if desired.

Discussion: Explore how it felt to freely apply the paint. Ask questions such as:

- Did you see an image in the mandala? Can you relate to it?

- Was it difficult to work in an unstructured manner, or was it fun and easy?

- Was applying the paint in this manner freeing or a chore?

- When was the last time you gave yourself permission to focus on yourself and do as you pleased?

- When was the last time you worked or played in an unrestricted manner?

Pointillism mandala[9]

Materials: Watercolor paper, acrylics, water, assortment of brushes.

Procedure: Explain the technique of pointillism: "A technique of painting in which small, distinct dots of pure color are applied in patterns to form an image." Georges Seurat developed the technique in 1886, branching from Impressionism. The technique relies on the ability of the eye and mind of the viewer to blend the color spots into a fuller range of tones.

Pointillism uses tiny dots instead of broad strokes to put the paint on the canvas. The concept of pointillism is to create solid space by using dots of two or more colors in an area. The colors mix from a distance, creating a new color. Landscapes were drawn in pencil first and then filled with the colored dots.

Next suggest that clients try to create a design using dots instead of brush strokes to create images.

Discussion: Examine the manner in which the dots create the image. Explore the idea of using tiny parts to create a whole. Generalize this theme to everyday life. Explore how taking tiny steps towards a goal will eventually lead to the goal; although it will take longer, the process will be less overwhelming. The outcome will most likely be the same or better because of the decreased stress.

Initial mandala[10]

Materials: Drawing paper, scissors, glue, markers, crayons, and oil pastels.

Procedure: Pre-print each participant a copy of the first initial of their first name (or they may draw their initial on drawing paper). Initials may be designed by using Microsoft Word; the initial should almost fill an entire 8½″×11″ (22×28cm) (A4) sheet of paper. Instruct clients to cut out the initial and then glue it within a pre-outlined circle. Next ask clients to create a background that reflects their personality. They may use words, images, shapes, and color, and small magazine photos.

Discussion: Focus on the images, symbolism, and colors utilized. Explore self-awareness, self-esteem, and personality characteristics. Discuss what makes each person valuable and unique.

Daydreams

Materials: Paints, brushes, water, magazine photos, glue, scissors, and oil pastels, markers, colored pencils, and crayons.

Procedure: Instruct group members to use a variety of media to represent daydreams, wishes, and fantasies.

Discussion: Discuss the significance of the symbols and images. Explore whether or not the clients believe their daydreams may eventually turn into reality, and, if so, examine methods to achieve goals. Explore the benefits and problems associated with daydreaming, and ask clients how their musings represent their personality, hopes, goals, attitudes, and behavior.

Explore the following questions:

- Do you allow yourself the time to daydream?

- Has daydreaming helped you cope with reality?

- Can you *hear* what your dreams are trying to tell you?

- Do your thoughts motivate you to try something new or change life patterns?

- Do you feel relaxed or comforted when you daydream?

Notes

1   A variation of this project is to have clients sponge paint to music or sounds (e.g. birds chirping, horns blowing, rustling of leaves). They may use colors and shapes which represent the sounds they hear.

2   www.babylon.com; http://artsmarts4kids.blogspot.com/2007/09/impressionism.html; and http://www.merriam-webster.com/dictionary/impressionism, all accessed July 13, 2012.

3   Fabric paint can be purchased from ssww.com (S&S art supplies).

4   Yolanda Brand. The introduction to this project may be edited according to the functioning of the clients.

5   Finger painting can cause anxiety and regression so it is important to determine if finger painting is appropriate for the population you are working with at the time.

6   This project is easy and non-threatening. It is a useful exercise for the non-compliant or defensive client.

7   Fiona Stolze, Inspired Art and Living, http://fionastolze.com/, accessed July 13, 2012. This project is complicated and would best be used with high functioning adults who have the ability to work in a complex, detailed manner. The project is geared for small groups or individual work (1–1), and would likely be broken up into a few sessions.

8   From en.wikipedia.org/wiki/Jackson_Pollock, accessed July 13, 2012 and Artcyclopedia (www.artcyclopedia.com). Artists by Movement. www.artcyclopedia.com/history/pointillism.html, accessed July 13, 2012.

9   Artcyclopedia, Artists by Movement: Pointillism, www.artcyclopedia.com/history/pointillism.html, accessed July 13, 2012.

10 Initials can be copied at http://printerprojects.com/alphabet/, accessed July 13, 2012.

Chapter 4

Mandala Collage

Mandala collage work allows clients to express themselves freely using a variety of resources. They are able to experiment with texture and touch, and to manipulate materials such as paper, photos, magazine pictures, fabric, foam shapes, felt, wood pieces, beads, construction paper, pipe cleaners, cotton, and shells, etc. Collages may be presented in numerous ways. A theme may be offered; specific materials may be used, and the collage might be structured or non-structured. A structured approach might include having group members use a theme for their collage such as emotions, designed by cutting out pictures of faces from magazines. A more non-structured approach might include having clients use a variety of materials such as wool and beads to represent inner feelings.

Individuals usually enjoy creating magazine collages because the pictures are easily accessible and there is no right or wrong way to do this exercise. The photos just need to be torn or cut out. Clients have an array of ideas right in front of them. They can find photos representing their feelings, family members, hobbies, likes and dislikes, and just glue them within the circle in any way they please.

The collage mandalas are non-threatening ways of representing thoughts, concerns, attitudes, and feelings. Clients usually feel free to share symbols represented in the collages. It is noteworthy to observe how clients create the collages, whether they are full or empty, organized or disorganized, glued neatly or haphazardly. The therapist can observe fine motor skills by the way in which the client cuts, and glues his pictures on the paper. The therapist gains extra knowledge about the client by the way in which he arranges the contents of the collages.

Mixed media collage

Materials: Tissue paper, 12″×18″ (30×45cm) drawing paper, scissors, glue, etc.

Procedure: Use a variety of materials including tissue paper, foam pieces, construction paper, Styrofoam™, buttons, felt, magazine pictures, glitter, sequins, etc. to create a collage within the mandala, which expresses a feeling, e.g. anger, happiness, anxiety, etc.

Discussion: Explore feelings and concerns. Discuss how the design and materials used represent various emotions.

Figure 63
Mandala illustrated in the color insert

A 55-year-old woman named Patty, diagnosed with schizoaffective disorder, designed this very organized mandala. She carefully placed the small foam pieces in order so that they would form a specific pattern. It was striking to observe that while she was working on this creation she appeared very tired and sometimes seemed to fall asleep for minutes at a time. Yet she would wake up, become clearer, and continue her work. Patty appeared to enjoy fitting the pieces together. She stated that the colors were pretty and she liked that they were so small. She saw it as a challenge, "It's like doing a puzzle."

Patty related the mandala to her own life. She stated she was finally feeling a little better and putting the pieces of her life back together. She had a boyfriend whom she was very fond of and a child she adored. Patty stated she used to think she was "nothing," but now feels better about herself. She stated that when she was in school the other children would tease her all the time and "sometimes push her around." They made fun of her because she was obese. Patty didn't understand why the kids were so cruel and why people are often so cruel to her now. She didn't understand why appearance was/is so important. She acted in a sheepish manner when group members complimented her artwork. Her self-esteem still needs much work, but she was able to thank her peers for their support.

Cut shapes

Materials: Construction paper, origami paper, glue, and scissors.

Procedure: Clients cut or tear a variety of shapes from construction paper and/or colorful origami paper and glue inside the circle in any way they please until a design is formed.

Discussion: Explore colors, shapes, and organization of the mandala. Encourage participants to relate the overall design to their mood and feelings. Examine how the organization of the mandala relates to the way clients organize their life. For example: Is the mandala balanced? Is their life in balance? Is the mandala disorganized? Is this reflective of the client's life? Does it appear chaotic, are there patterns, etc.?

Figure 64
Mandala illustrated in the color insert

A 37-year-old client named Janey designed this colorful mandala. The mandala took three sessions to complete because of the entire cutting, gluing, and details incorporated into it. Janey was very satisfied with its outcome. Some of the shapes were pre-drawn. Janey cut them out and colored them in, others she designed by herself. She stated the mandala represented her brighter mood, now that she was recovering from her depression. Most of the colors are quite vivid except for 2–3 areas of a darker blue (remnants of her depression). Janey liked the mandala because it symbolized happiness and movement. She was hoping to get back to work and to become more involved with her current boyfriend, whom she had been ignoring for the last few months. She stated that the red flower (off center) represented growth and pleasure; the leaf under it represented autumn/change, and the blue squiggly line towards the bottom of the page symbolized the ups and downs of life. The orange shape under the red flower has a small pink shape within it. When asked about this presentation, she said it represented her desire to have a baby. Her goals were to eventually marry her current boyfriend, go on a honeymoon to Hawaii, and then try to have a child. She stated her time "is running out."

Figure 65

Pam, a woman in her 20s, included a vivid burst of color emanating from a central point to represent positive thoughts about her recovery from depression. She stated the bright and detailed designs represented her uniqueness and desire to "stand out in a crowd." She felt very strongly about wanting do something exceptional in life, and was hoping to become a successful writer. She saw herself as bold and bright, ready to take on challenges in her life. Pam was supported for her optimism and positive goals, but it was suggested she might slow down a little bit and take one step at a time. She had a habit of doing too much at once, becoming overwhelmed after a short while and falling into depression.

Figure 66
Mandala illustrated in the color insert

Victoria, a woman in her 40s carefully worked on this mandala she titled "Inside Out." Victoria related the mandala to her world "as it is at the moment." She stated the designs and the shapes reminded her of material, "like a shirt," that is inside out. The circles on top of the wavy lines reminded her of aimless floating. Victoria remarked that she feels like she is aimlessly floating; she doesn't have a clue where she is going in life or who she really is. She doesn't want to remain married to her husband and she dislikes her job. She stated she wants to move to a new apartment because hers is too small and uncomfortable. She sees herself in a sort of limbo. Victoria was attracted to the stars (center circle). She related the stars to aspirations for the future and hope that maybe her life will improve.

Movie poster mandala[1]

Materials: Photos of current and past movie posters, glue, scissors, and markers.

Procedure: The group leader creates booklets filled with movie poster photos; each photo would be approximately 3″×2″ (8×5cm), but sizes could vary. Clients are given the booklets and asked to cut out a variety of posters that appeal to them. Next they glue the posters within the circle to create a unique collage. The photos can be cut to fit exactly within the circle or placed in a random manner. Designs and color may be added with markers if desired.

Discussion: Clients share the movies chosen, their reaction to the movies, and memories elicited from the movies and related discussions.

Figure 67
Mandala illustrated in the color insert

A young woman named Elyse stated she had been experiencing anxiety and depression since her boyfriend of two years chose to end their relationship. She was devastated that their feelings about each other weren't reciprocal. Elyse was "crazy about him" she had thought they would eventually marry, have children, and live happily ever after. Unfortunately, he had stopped calling her every day, as he had in the past, and he began making excuses on date nights. He would say he had to visit a friend or work late. She had noticed he was acting aloof and strange. Finally she confronted him and he told her that he had fallen out of love and wanted to see other people. He did want to remain friends, an idea that was unacceptable to Elyse. Elyse was shocked and distraught, and this rejection, along with a history of depression, might have led to her recent suicide attempt by swallowing too many barbiturates while drinking wine.

Elyse appeared pleased to work on this project and decided the theme of her mandala would be "relationships." There were many mini posters to choose from, but she made sure to only choose those that included love between two people. *Casablanca* was in the center because that was her favorite movie and she admired the relationship between Humphrey Bogart and Ingrid Bergman. *The Addams Family* poster made her giggle as she stated she liked when Gomez kissed Morticia up the arm. *Rocky*, she said, made her cry, "but a good cry." *You've Got Mail* was a favorite because she liked the way the relationship developed throughout the movie between Tom Hanks and Meg Ryan. Elyse envied the way the star's feelings for each other grew over time, from hate to true love. Another favorite was *50 First Dates*, which she saw many times. She sighed and stated that she wished a man would love her the way Adam Sandler loved and pursued Drew Barrymore "even though she was disabled." Elyse also added *Along Came Polly*, saying that Ben Stiller was adorable and worked so hard to win over Polly (Jennifer Aniston). "He even tried to dance although he was opposed to it at first; he wanted to please her." Elyse remarked that she liked her mandala; it helped remind her that maybe there was still time to meet someone wonderful. When prompted, she decided to name the mandala "My Desire."

Animal mandala

Materials: Outlines of various animals including birds, dogs, cats, lions, owls, snakes, etc., glue, scissors, makers, oil pastels, and crayons.

Procedure: Provide group members with a booklet filled with an assortment of animal outlines. Each animal should be duplicated about six times. The pictures should be small enough so that six of them could fit neatly into a circle the size of a typical paper plate. Instruct participants to decide which animal they prefer or relate to the most, and then have them create a mandala using at least one animal outline in their design. Clients may divide the mandala into segments and glue the animal outlines within the segments, creating a pattern, or they may keep the mandala whole and glue the animals toward the center or borders of the mandala, which would create a more random design. Next participants should color in their animal outline and create an environment around it.

Discussion: Explore the animals chosen and their significance. Discuss how participants relate to the behaviors and characteristics of the animals. Examine what clients can learn from animals in regards to strength, endurance, coping skills, life style, and survival.

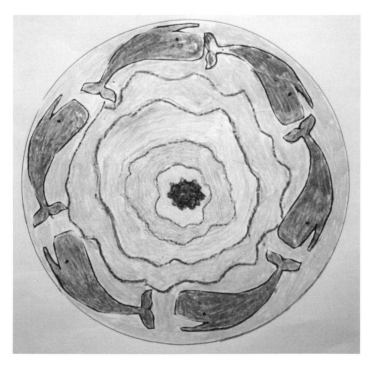

Figure 68

A 40-year-old woman named Christine chose to include dolphins in her mandala design. The dolphins appear to look like whales but Christine chose to view them as dolphins. She stated that she and the dolphins have similar characteristics: "They are smart, like to be with a group, enjoy having fun, are playful, are silly at times and enjoy freedom." She also remarked that she loves the water and goes to the seashore as much as possible. Christine stated she is similar to the dolphins because she is almost always cheerful, "except in recent months," and "I used to smile a lot." She viewed the dolphins as strong and hopeful. Christine was trying to get pregnant, but was experiencing a lot of disappointment and discomfort. For two years she had been taking hormone injections that were costly and uncomfortable. She had three miscarriages during this period of time. Her great frustration about not conceiving soon turned into depression and anxiety. She began to isolate, and had trouble sleeping; she was overeating. "I gained 15 pounds in one month." She remarked that she felt a lot of pressure from her husband and his family to conceive. She reported that her husband had recently become irritable and ill tempered, losing his patience easily and frequently. She was fearful he might decide to leave her if she could not conceive. "This is my last chance," she exclaimed. She had married late in life and regretted postponing marriage and children. "I focused on my career and now I am sorry." She stated she felt selfish for "putting myself first." Christine believed that dolphins were a good omen, a sign that maybe she would have a baby in the upcoming year. She drew them circling a series of smaller circles. Inside the circles she placed a small, blue flower-like shape, which she called "the fetus." The circles surrounding the fetus were "protective." Christine mentioned "They are there to keep the baby safe and keep the dolphins from eating it." When asked to clarify what she meant, she stated that although the dolphins were friendly, "sometimes they turn on you, I can't take any chances." She then related the dolphins to her body, which she felt had been working against her.

Christine decided to use the mandala as a tool for prayer. She remarked that she would stare at it every day and wish for a baby. Christine whispered, "Maybe if I wish long enough my dream will come true."

Figure 69

Eric, a male in his 30s, diagnosed with bipolar disorder, designed this bright mandala. He decided to use a variety of animals in his design, "I couldn't choose just one." He chose a dolphin to represent "fun," a bird to represent "freedom and flying," a dog to represent "someone to love me," and a lady bug, "because I used to like playing with them when I was a kid." When asked which animal he could relate to the most, he remarked "the dog." Eric stated that he had a difficult life, a father who drank and had very unpredictable behavior. "You never knew when he would scream and hit you for no reason. I was always scared. But now I have a girlfriend whom I love. She does everything for me and I do everything for her. She loves my cooking and I like the fact that she cleans the house. I could be very sloppy, but she doesn't seem to mind. She picks up my dirty clothes and washes them. She is heavy, but she has a good soul, that is what is really important."

Eric stated that dogs are loved unconditionally, and he is thrilled that his girlfriend loves *him* unconditionally. "No matter how I look or what I do, even when 'I am crazy' she loves me. I dye my hair, and I'm losing it, but she doesn't care." He added a star in the center of the mandala to represent happiness, and a small sun in the upper right hand corner to represent hope. Eric felt the small sun wasn't emphasized enough, so he decided to surround the circle with a yellow border and create a sun mandala. He stated the sun represented his joyfulness and gratitude. Eric remarked he could have kept "adding and adding" to his mandala, which is quite busy (a sign of his hypomania). He was very pleased with the outcome of the mandala and excited to share it with group members.

Figure 70

Dan, a male in his early 30s who had been diagnosed with schizoaffective disorder, was a friendly, outgoing, lively individual.[2] He was a pleasure to have in the art therapy sessions because he was focused, involved, and encouraged his peers to participate. He was genuinely interested in helping others as well as himself. He chose a cat as the focus of his mandala. Dan enjoyed cartooning and creating make-believe stories, so he called the cat "Secret Agent Cat." He attempted to make the cat's coat look like a trench coat.

He stated, "Secret agent cat goes on many adventures and captures the crooks; he has a lot of fun." Dan saw certain similarities between himself and the cat. In a light hearted manner he remarked that they both "are funny, like to wear trench coats, and like to explore." He also remarked that he loves cats and has one named Bonkers at home.

The cat is the focus of the mandala. It is large and its eyes, though small, are peering at the observer. The head is carefully colored in, but the coat is filled in, in a haphazard manner. There is a sun to the right, almost centered above the cat's head.

Dan enjoyed joking and being the center of attention. He displayed a good sense of humor and always had a smile on his face. Some of his good humor seemed to be a façade because when he went home he would often become panicky and hear voices, which would upset him and keep him awake at night. He was a very large man. The scribbled coat may represent the lack of focus on the body because losing weight was a big issue for him. The peering eyes may represent hallucinations and fears. Dan seemed to be hiding behind his comicalness, and the cat hides under the trench coat. The coat gives the cat power; much like Dan's humor does for him. The cat is naked, just a cat, under its trench coat, and Dan is naked in a sense, a frightened man beneath his façade. The cat seemed to give him a sense of control and importance, a way to live vicariously, through the cat's adventures.

Love myself collage mandala

Materials: Drawing paper or construction paper, magazines, construction paper, tissue paper, felt, sequins and other collage materials, scissors, glue, and markers.

Procedure: Ask group members to find pictures that represent ways to nurture, soothe, and show love and respect for oneself. In addition, participants might choose to cut out a variety of shapes such as hearts and flowers from construction and/or tissue paper. They might use words from the magazines to help emphasize thoughts. Photos might include healthy and/or delicious food, people smiling, families showing affection, people enjoying vacations, someone sipping tea, etc.

Discussion/goals: Clients discuss the positive photos that comprise the collage and their associations to the photos. Goals include increased self-esteem and identification of ways to cherish oneself.

Figure 71

Rosa, a woman in her 40s, focused on positive people and events in her life. She emphasized parties, her ten-year-old dog George, her family (including her mother, father, husband and daughter), dolls (which she loved in the past and her daughter adores now), a warm, sunny day, the ocean, and technology. She shared that she enjoys swimming and sunning at the beach. Rosa stated that family picnics and functions are her favorite activity. She remarked that the support her family provides and her deep love for her husband and daughter "is what keeps me going." She spoke about her mother (center of circle: woman with gray hair) who is ill with cancer. Rosa stated that her mother provides strength and is her role model. She prays for her every night and knows she will recover. When asked if Rosa would like to describe her mother she bellowed "She's amazing, beautiful and always there for me."

My history

Materials: Markers, crayons, pastels, drawing paper, magazines, glue, and scissors.

Procedure: Instruct clients to utilize photos from magazines and personal photos, if desired, to create a grouping of pictures within the circle that reflect various aspects of their life from youth to adulthood. They may also add words and illustrations.

Discussion/goals: Discussion focuses on life experiences and the role past experiences and relationships have on one's present mood, behavior, and feelings. Goals include reminiscing and self-awareness.

Tissue paper collage

Materials: Tissue paper, scissors, glue, 11″×14″ (28×35cm) drawing paper, and construction paper.

Procedure: Pieces of tissue paper, in a variety of sizes, colors, and shapes, may be provided, or clients may tear and/or cut the paper themselves from large sheets. The tissue paper pieces are then glued onto the mandala. The resulting design may be abstract, or the client may choose to create a more realistic image such as a butterfly or flower.

Discussion: Problem solving and decision making is focused upon. Discussion centers on the meaning of the colors chosen and the way the clients chose to place the tissue paper within the circle. The feelings evoked by the colors may be explored.

Magazine collage: Self-portrait[3]

Materials: Magazines, scissors, glue, and paper.

Procedure: Clients cut or tear pictures from magazines that they identify with or admire. They may want to select pictures which represent their likes, dislikes, surroundings, family, and friends. The pictures are then glued onto the mandala. Clients may use markers to add any word or picture that is unavailable to them in the magazines.

Discussion/goals: Exploring self-awareness and self-esteem, expressing a variety of feelings in a non-threatening manner.

Memory collage

Materials: Magazines, scissors, glue, drawing paper, and construction paper.

Procedure: Clients cut and paste magazine photos within the mandala to represent special occasions, events, and important people in their lives. They may use personal photos and/or memorabilia in addition to the magazine pictures.

Discussion/goals: Individuals discuss their past and how their past affects their present actions, feelings, and attitudes. The activity enhances one's self-awareness. It is a favorite activity for the older client.

Calming collage

Materials: Magazines, glue, drawing paper, and scissors.

Procedure: Clients are asked to cut or tear pictures which give them a feeling of peacefulness. They are asked to glue the pictures onto the mandala.

A full body relaxation exercise might precede the art experience. The clients may then be asked to design a collage of the serenity they felt during the relaxation exercise.

Discussion: Methods of attaining a peaceful state of mind and stress reduction techniques are explored.

A collage of feelings

Materials: Magazines, construction paper, drawing paper, collage materials such as pom poms, feathers, sequins, pipe cleaners, scissors, and glue.

Procedure: Ask clients to create a design that represents one or more feelings or emotions.

Discussion/goals: Discussion focuses on the feeling/emotion chosen and the way it is represented in the collage. Goals include problem solving, focusing, increased self-awareness, and self-expression.

Shapes[4]

Materials: Drawing paper, construction paper, glue, scissors, markers, crayons, and oil pastels.

Procedure: Group members choose one piece of construction paper, which will be used as their base. Have them choose the color that best represents their mood. Next clients cut out a variety of shapes from the drawing paper and fill them in with color, lines and images. The shapes are cut out and glued within the circle to create a design that reflects the artist's mood, feelings, and/or personality characteristics.

Discussion: Participants share the personal message conveyed by the mandala. Self-awareness and self-esteem is focused upon.

Life experience collage

Materials: Magazines, scissors, glue, and mandala.

Procedure: Clients are encouraged to cut or tear pictures from magazines which they find meaningful. They may choose pictures which they can relate to, and which symbolize various parts of their life (e.g. a young couple holding hands might represent a special relationship, mountains might represent a favorite vacation). Participants may cut out words, letters, and advertisements. The pictures are then glued onto the mandala.

Discussion/goals: Discussion focuses on the images chosen, the way the pictures are placed within the circle, and their meaning. Clients explore goals, self-esteem, and thoughts about significant people and events in their life. Degree of satisfaction with their life is explored as well as methods to promote positive change.

Inner body collage[5]

Materials: Construction paper, scissors, glue, a variety of textured materials: cotton, buttons, feathers, pom poms, burlap, etc.

Procedure: Encourage clients to close their eyes and relax. Guide a relaxation exercise, having clients tighten and relax the muscles throughout their body (from their head down to their toes). Encourage clients to try to *feel* and visualize their inner body and how it functions (e.g. have them listen to the beating of their heart and then visualize what their heart, lungs, kidneys, etc. look like). When clients have relaxed, opened their eyes, and taken a deep breath, have them create a collage depicting the way their insides felt during the relaxation experience. They may also represent how they think their insides (organs) look.

Discussion/goals: Becoming more familiar with bodily processes, inner as well as outer; exploring how inner body feelings reflect feelings about oneself, self-awareness.

Music inspired collage

Materials: Music tapes, mandala, magazines, scissors, and glue.

Procedure: Play recordings of classical or romantic music (or whatever music is suitable for the population you are working with at the time). Have the clients close their eyes, relax, and *feel* the music. Have them imagine that they see the music: the shapes, colors, and movement of the music. Next suggest that they look through the magazines and cut out pictures that relate to the music they just listened to. Encourage participants to glue the pictures within the mandala to symbolize their experience.

Discussion: Clients focus on expressing feelings and emotions. They might explore ways in which music and meditation relax them and can be used as effective stress reduction techniques.

Mandala collage

Materials: Paper plate, drawing paper, construction paper, markers, scissors, glue, and magazines.

Procedure: Clients use a plate to trace a circle onto white drawing paper or construction paper. They are instructed to fill in the circle with pictures from magazines that they find meaningful. They may title the mandala if they so desire.

Discussion/goals: Discussion focuses on the meaning of the collage and the manner in which it is designed. Goals include focusing, centering, problem solving, and expression of feelings.

Relaxation exercise and mandala collage

Materials: Cardboard circles, collage materials (e.g. feathers, pipe cleaners, pom poms, buttons, etc.), scissors, glue, and markers.

Procedure: The group facilitator leads a simple relaxation exercise. Clients are invited to relax, close their eyes and take a few deep breaths. Starting from their head to their toes have them tighten and relax various parts of their body. They might be asked to tighten and then relax their eyes, nose, mouth, neck, shoulders, arms, hands, stomach, buttocks, legs, feet, and toes. When the exercise is over ask clients to create a collage mandala representing the peaceful state they felt during the relaxation experience.

Discussion/goals: Discussion focuses on the way in which the collage represents tranquility for each individual. Goals include focusing, abstract thinking, exploration of relaxation techniques and coping skills.

Colored paper collage

Materials: Drawing paper, paper plates, construction paper and various types of decorative paper (glossy, patterned, origami paper), glue, and scissors.

Procedure: Ask clients to cut out various colored shapes that evoke a peaceful feeling. Instruct clients to glue these shapes onto the mandala in any way they choose.

Discussion: Discussion focuses on examining the serene shapes and colors. Explore ways clients can find peace and serenity in their life.

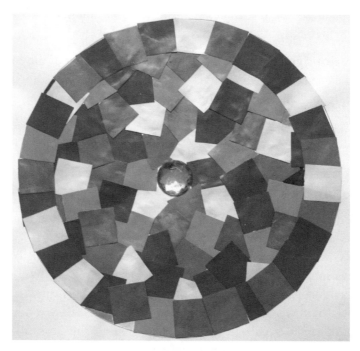

Figure 72
Mandala illustrated in the color insert

Harriet, a woman in her 70s, overcoming severe depression, worked methodically to design this well-balanced and well-thought-out mandala. She began on the periphery, carefully and slowly working her way towards the center. When the mandala was completed she added the stone in the center. It took Harriet a few weeks to complete the mandala and almost an entire session just to decide the color of the center stone. Harriet was immersed in this project. She continued it even when her peers had completed their projects and were working on something else. She stated she found it relaxing and was in no hurry to "move on." She remarked she would work on the mandala until she was satisfied that it was completed; she did not succumb to peer pressure. Harriet found that listening to soothing music while she worked was very relaxing. She became a little anxious, though, as she began working towards the center of the mandala, because the small paper squares had to be manipulated in order to fit in the space according to her specifications. Harriet was able to relate the mandala to her personality because she characterized herself as a perfectionist, wanting order in her house and order in her life. She remarked that she becomes off balanced when things go wrong in her life. A major goal for Harriet was to try to deal more effectively with life's obstacles and inevitable changes.

Mandala of textures

Materials: Bag full of items (see below), glue, and drawing paper.

Procedure: Present a bag or box full of items that have distinct textures, such as sandpaper, Brillo™ soap pads, corduroy material, ridge potato chips, or bristles on a small brush. Ask clients to choose a variety of items and take some time experiencing them (touching them, focusing on how they look, feel, smell, etc.). Suggest that clients glue the textured objects on the mandala to form a design.

Discussion: Discussion focuses on the significance of touch in our relationships and in our environment. Clients may share how touch can affect mood and stress levels (for example, petting a cat or dog often relieves anxiety and lowers blood pressure). Being in the moment allows an individual to fully enjoy the experience and reap many rewards.

Peace, love, diversity

Materials: Poster board, markers, scissors, glue, felt and construction paper, assorted materials such as sequins, feathers, pom poms, colored macaroni pieces, small paper squares, magazine photos, etc.

Procedure: Suggest clients create a mandala by using symbols representing what peace, love, and diversity means to them. Encourage group members to utilize a variety of materials in their design.

Discussion: Explore the meaning of the mandalas and how their unique messages affect participant's attitudes, behavior, relationships, and satisfaction with life.

Arrow collage mandala

Materials: Construction paper, drawing paper, scissors, glue, markers, and cardboard.

Procedure: Clients cut a variety of arrows (all shapes, sizes, and colors) from construction paper. (The client can draw the arrows or the therapist may draw and cut them out beforehand if this is an issue.) At least 4–6 arrows per person are needed. Group participants are asked to arrange the arrows within the circle in such a way that they represent the direction of one's life (e.g. Are all the arrows pointing downwards? Are they going in many different directions?). The arrows are then glued onto the paper or cardboard.

Discussion/goals: Discussion focuses on exploring one's life direction, goals, and obstacles to achieving one's goals. Objectives include achieving greater self-awareness, focusing, and problem solving.

A woman in her 40s named Lori, who was diagnosed with bipolar disorder, created this multidirectional mandala. Lori seemed to have fun with this project, coloring and cutting the arrows carefully and creatively. She worked diligently while filling in the arrows, using various shading and design techniques. When it was time to adhere the arrows, Lori let loose, and appeared to glue them quickly, without much thought. This was in direct contrast to the way she approached the first half of the project. Lori stated that she purposely arranged the arrows to go in different directions because they represented the confusion she was experiencing. She felt that she was going around in circles and getting nowhere. She didn't have goals and believed that she had not accomplished anything in her 43 years of life. She had difficulty maintaining relationships and keeping a job. Her family was annoyed with her for being irresponsible and always pleading with them for money. Lori tended to spend her disability check the minute she received it; she didn't ration her money, and often didn't have enough money for food, toiletries, or bus fare during the second half of the month. She had been married for three years, but her husband divorced her because of her moodiness and unpredictable outbursts. She was not always medication compliant. Lori mentioned that she does not know "what her life direction is" and feels badly about this confusion and uncertainty. When asked about the size of the arrows, she replied that the largest, thickest arrow is in the center, pointing straight up. She said this was the first arrow she placed on the paper. She was able to relate it to her hope for a brighter future even though she felt depressed and hopeless. When asked about her use of color (the shades are very vivid) she stated she loves bright hues and she likes to wear dazzling colors, "They make me feel better."

The mandala clearly represented Lori's hypomanic state as well as her confusion in regards to future plans and direction. It provided her a safe way to explore her feelings, observe the reality of her situation, and then work on ways to outline strategies to attain possible goals.

Colored tape mandala

Materials: Colored tape in various widths, scissors, and glue.

Procedure: Participants use an assortment of colored tape to create a design within the mandala.

Discussion: Participants share associations to the colors and artwork. Explore the degree of detail utilized. Further discussion may entail focusing on the tape and relating the *sticky tape* to *sticky* (tricky, uncomfortable, problematic) situations clients might have experienced in the past and the methods used to resolve them.

Sunburst mandala

Materials: Drawing paper, construction paper, glue, scissors, and markers.

Procedure: Clients outline a circle from a small circular template such as the top of a coffee can. They are asked to fill in the circle with colors and shapes that are self-representative. Next clients will cut out strips of white or colored paper, about ½" (1cm) thick, so that the strips are radiating (like sun's rays) from the center circle. They will glue these strips all around the center circle. Next participants will write positive characteristics, achievements, and strengths in the rays.

Discussion: Explore the energy emanated from the rays and ways in which the mandala promotes positive thinking, hope, and self-esteem. Examine each participant's unique qualities and worthiness.

Everyday object life collage

Materials: Cardboard circle, scissors, glue gun or strong glue, objects used in everyday life such as Band-Aids, Brillo pads, toothbrush, small cereal box label, Q-tips™, cotton balls, etc.

Procedure: Participants and/or the group leader bring in an array of small common objects that are used frequently by most people. Next clients choose and then glue the objects within the circle to form an artistic portrayal of their everyday life.

Discussion: Participants talk about the items chosen and their placement within the circle. Have them answer the following question: "What do you need to be content and feel well, and to lead a healthy lifestyle?"

The past

Materials: Poster board, markers, oil pastels, magazine photos, personal photos, personal trinkets that can be glued on poster board, glue, and scissors.

Procedure: Instruct participants to find magazine photos, draw images and designs, and include words and phrases that represent their past. They may also use personal items to glue onto the mandala.

Discussion: Explore the images, photos, objects, and words that compose the mandala. Examine how group members feel about their past and the effect it has had on their present mood, feelings, and behavior. Examine the best and worst parts of their history, and pose questions such as:

- Would you go back in time if you could?

- What age would you like to be?

- What was one of your best experiences? Worst experiences?

- Do you end to focus more on the past, present or future? Does this help or hurt you?

- What have you learned from the past that you could apply to the present?

- How can you use the past to make your present more pleasant?

States[6]

Materials: Outlines of the 50 states of the United States. Drawing paper, scissors, glue, markers, crayons, colored pencils, and oil pastels.

Procedure: Have clients share which state they view as their *home state* and ask them to describe something unique about it. Provide an outline of each state chosen. Instruct clients to create a person, animal, image, or design from the outline. Suggest they think of images representing their childhood and/or thoughts about growing up in that state. Next direct participants to cut out their state outline and glue it within the mandala. A background may be added.

Discussion: Clients examine how the mandala symbolism relates to personality characteristics, thoughts about childhood, and attitudes towards one's home state, environment, and community.

Figure 73
Mandala illustrated in the color insert

A 23-year-old woman named Annette, who was challenged with depression and anxiety, created this symbolic mandala. Annette had been experiencing severe panic attacks and insomnia. A recent college graduate, she was not sure what she wanted to do with her life and felt overwhelmed. Annette was from New Jersey and chose to represent herself as a Spanish dancer. Her outline (the State of New Jersey) was drawn on the computer, filled in with color, and used as the focal point of the mandala. Annette remarked that she enjoyed living in New Jersey because it was pretty, near the shore, and close to Philadelphia and Manhattan. She stated that she designed a Spanish dancer because she had a Spanish pen pal, studied Spanish in school, wanted to visit Spain, and adored all types of dancing. She mentioned that she used to pretend she was a well-known artist, dancing on the Broadway stage. She stated that she found this type of "pretending" relaxing and comforting. Symbols in the background of the mandala include a sun with electric rays, colorful flowers blossoming, and a dark red boot shoe with two mini "fairies" dancing on it, a yellow diamond towards the top of the circle and cross hatched lines on either side of the figure. Annette shared that the symbols represented various aspects of her personality. She characterized herself as anxious (the sun's rays), feeling a little better (the growing flowers), and enjoying attention (the diamond and focus on the figure). On the left side of the circle a tiny fairy is situated under a rain cloud. Annette mentioned that the figure represented herself when she was in the throes of a deep depression, feeling helpless and hopeless. The rain represented her tears. The fairy is seen walking away from the rain cloud and climbing rocks and a gray mountain until she arrives at the shoe, and views the stars, "which are the next step." The stars lead to the flowers and represent "freedom." Annette viewed the mandala as "complicated, but hopeful."

Figure 74
Mandala illustrated in the color insert

Bits and pieces

Materials: Drawing paper, markers, scissors, and glue.

Procedure: Clients fill in the circle with magazine photos and/or drawings that answer the question, "What makes life worth living?" Examples may include items such as ice cream, children, family, a sunset, people holding hands, eating, etc.

Discussion: Explore the objects chosen. Discuss their placement and order of importance. Examine if participants have the things they need at the moment. If not, explore ways to attain desires and goals.

Notes

1   Movie posters to copy and print may be found on Google Images or www.art.com (ensure they are copyright free images).

2   Sadly, Dan passed away before this publication was completed. He was a wonderful man with a good heart and will be remembered fondly.

3   Other variations of this project may include designing happiness, anger, and word collages (clients cut out meaningful words and sentences from magazines).

4   Shapes that are pre-outlined and ready to be colored in may also be utilized.

5   This art therapy experience is a modified version of a workshop I took part in during Pratt's 1981 Creative Arts Therapy Expo.

6   Outlines can be found on Google Images. An outline of countries, such as England, may be utilized.

Chapter 5

Group Work

Group mandala work is beneficial because socialization and communication skills are enhanced. When individuals work together a new element is added to mandala design. The colors, symbols, and details are even more complex and exciting. Problem solving and flexibility become very important because everyone works together to make creative decisions. Clients examine how they interact with others and how others interact with them. The mandala becomes a representation of everyone in the group and unity is achieved.

One's role in therapy group often relates to one's role in family and/or other social relationships. If an individual is quiet and withdrawn during group work he often shares that he is also reserved with friends, family, etc. Observing and examining this communication style allows the individual to better understand his relationship style and communication problems with significant people in his life.

Group work is frequently less threatening than individual work. The client is not singled out, as he may feel he is when he shares his individual artwork. He is not solely responsible for the outcome of the artwork; the entire group is the artist. Many individuals find comfort in this and enjoy working with peers while sharing thoughts and ideas. The combination of the safety of the circular mandala and the effort by all participants makes this type of work appealing for even the most defiant client.

Mandala mural I

Materials: Mural paper or cardboard, paper plates, oil pastels, pastels, and acrylic paint.

Procedure: Each group member traces a circle from a paper plate, and creates his own unique mandala. When the mandalas are completed they are all glued on one large sheet of mural paper for exploration and review.

Discussion/goals: Discussion focuses on the design, significance, and placement of the mandalas. Goals include centering, socialization, sharing with others, defining, and recognizing boundaries.

Mandala mural II[1]

Materials: Large template such as garbage can lid, markers, paints, and oil pastels.

Procedure: Clients work together to design one large mandala. They may work at the same time or take turns.

Discussion: Clients share thoughts about the ease or difficulty of working together. Group members acknowledge each others' contributions and work together to critique the overall design of the mandala. Cooperation and mutual respect is emphasized.

Figure 75
Mandala illustrated in the color insert

One intention of the mandala is to embody wholeness and
unity. This mandala was created prior to moving the art studio
to a different room. To ease the transition, it was explained that
we would be creating a unity mandala for the new studio space.
Each group member could contribute a design or pattern, as a
way to bring unity experienced in the old room with us into the
new room.

Figure 76

Four mature female clients created this mandala. They decided to
divide the circle up into four sections so they could each work
on their own segment as opposed to working in unison. The two
clients who worked on the right side of the mandala chose a mostly
spiral theme. It is noteworthy that these two women were much
more social and animated than the other two clients. They giggled,
joked, and sometimes seemed to irritate the other two women, who
appeared deep in thought. The mood of the women is demonstrated
in the intensity, color, and detail of their designs. The boisterous
clients put more effort in their work than the other two women did.

The artist who filled in the flower segment on the left side was quiet but involved. The artist who filled in the segment on the lower left part of the circle was participatory but in an obligatory manner. She wanted to do what she was instructed to do, no more, no less. She stated, when asked, that the flowers she drew were supposed to be the spirals copied from the other clients. She complained that they looked like lollipops as opposed to roses. When the mandala was completed the participants stated they were pleased with the outcome. They liked the way the yellow circle in the center brought it "all together." The women thought they worked well together and did not think there was a group leader. They believed that everyone was equal in the group and everyone did their best. The participants seemed pleased to hang the mandala on the wall of the art room where everyone could admire it. The women did say they liked working together because it took the onus off them to create a "pretty" piece of art. They said it was easier and more fun when they worked together.

Connections

Materials: Mural paper, scissors, glue, large circular template, construction paper, and markers.

Procedure: The leader or a group member uses a circular template (about the size of a large garbage can cover) to outline the mandala. Next clients cut out colorful strips of paper in varying sizes. After the strips are cut, suggest participants create a design where their strips interconnect with other members' strips so that all the pieces are linked in some way and an abstract design is formed.

Discussion/goals: Discussion focuses on connecting with others. Goals include socialization, problem solving, and cooperation among group members.

Clients greatly enjoyed this project. They asked if they could "do it all the time." One woman was surprised that she could contribute to such a beautiful piece of art. Another woman thought if the mandala was framed it could be hung up in the Museum of Modern Art. Even an elderly man, who normally didn't like to participate, felt comfortable adding to this construction. He was not worried about making mistakes or appearing foolish. His poor memory and inability to follow directions would usually make him leery about doing artwork. Clients remarked they felt calm and had fun while working. A few shared that while they worked they didn't think about their problems. They were in the moment. They enjoyed watching each other take turns and liked giving suggestions to each other about placement of the shapes. Most individuals enjoyed choosing the various colors and deciding the size of the strips (they had scissors so they could trim them). They liked deciding which strips should be adjoining, which strips should be used, and which should be discarded. Everyone was able to control how the design was created. They were so proud of the work that most participants chose to put their names within the mandala.

Figure 77

Group mandala I: Mini mandalas within a mandala

Materials: Mural paper, drawing paper, large circular template (about the size of a garbage can lid), small circular template (about the size of a coffee can lid) markers, crayons, oil pastels, and scissors.

Procedure: The group leader outlines the perimeter of a circle (about the size of a garbage can lid). Simultaneously, clients are instructed to outline the perimeter of a coffee can lid or similar item and cut it out. Next clients fill in the smaller circles with shapes, color, and images, etc. When all of the circles are completed group members cut them out and glue them within the larger circle in any way they please. Lastly, clients create an environment surrounding the mini mandalas.

Discussion: Participants explore the significance of the individual mini mandalas and the overall design of the large mandala that contains them. The theme of working together, connections, and being part of a community is discussed.

Mandala drawing pass

Materials: Drawing paper, paper plates, pencils, markers, oil pastels, and crayons.

Procedure: Clients outline a circle from a paper plate on drawing paper. They put their first name or initials on the bottom of the paper. Have them draw something on the mandala. After a minute or two have clients pass their mandala to the person on their right and that person adds to it. Eventually everyone has the chance to add to each other's mandala. This goes on until each group member has contributed something to each mandala. Clients should have their original work back and are then asked to title it and share his thoughts about all of the symbols added.

Discussion: Discussion focuses on the meaning the artist gives to his mandala and the various interpretations of the symbols. Emphasize that each mandala is the sum of everyone's work. Examine thoughts about flexibility and working as a team.

Group pizza mandala

Materials: Triangle shapes, like slices of pizza, cut from white drawing paper, markers, oil pastels, crayons, mural paper, and masking tape.

Procedure: Outline a large circle from a template. Then each group member receives a triangle "slice of pizza." The clients are instructed to fill in their triangles, creating their favorite type of pizza—sausage, pepperoni, spinach, etc. Then they place (tape) the individual pieces of pizza together so they form a circle (just like a real pizza pie).

Discussion: Each group member discusses his contribution to the pizza pie. The clients then explain ways in which the pizza is reflective of his personality, e.g. "Are you fancy, like a pepperoni and sausage, or plain and simple, like a cheese no sauce pie?" Self-esteem is focused upon.

Two person mandala I

Materials: Drawing paper, markers, oil pastels, and crayons.

Procedure: Clients divide into pairs and work together to create a mandala. They are instructed to divide the circle in half. Each individual is asked to fill in one half of the mandala in any way they please.

Discussion: Participants observe how the halves work together as a design. They explore similarities and/or differences in the artwork, specifically the colors, shapes, and figures. Examine the ease or difficulty of working with another person in this manner and the themes of acceptance, dealing with differences, opposites and unity. Explore how the two different sides of the mandala work to create a complete design, and how this idea can be applied to everyday life. (Differences in culture, traditions, religion, nationalities, and ideas can be celebrated and lead to harmony.)

"Patch of life" mandala

Materials: Mural paper, large circular template (approximately the size of a garbage can lid—about 20 inches (50cm) in diameter), markers, oil pastels, crayons, construction paper, scissors, and glue.

Procedure: Each participant receives a 3″×3″ (8×8cm) or 4″×4″ (10×10cm) square of paper. The size of the square will depend on how many people are participating. The squares will need to fit into the mandala. The group leader uses a template to outline a very large circle (about 20″ (50cm) in diameter). Everyone chooses a paper color. Clients will be asked to draw one patch of their life (one part of it) on the paper. When the pictures are completed, clients decide together as a group where to place them within the circle, and then they are glued to create a mandala quilt.

Discussion/goals: Discussion focuses on the quilt and each individual's representational square. Goals include socialization, sharing, group cohesion, and increased self-esteem by being part of a team.

Welcome mandala

Materials: Drawing paper, markers, oil pastels, and crayons, and large mandala template.

Procedure: Ask group members to work together to draw and/or cut out figures, symbols, pictures, and words that are welcoming for newcomers to the group. Examples include: smiling faces, suns, flowers, trees, people holding hands, the word "welcome" written in a decorative manner, etc. The images and photos are then glued or drawn within the mandala.

Discussion: Discussion focuses on the drawings and pictures, and the way in which they represent a warm welcome for new group members. Group members are supported to share their contributions to the mandala and their thoughts about working together.

Unity mandala

Materials: Drawing paper, large circular outlined from a template approximately 18″–20″ (46–50cm) in diameter, glue sticks, markers, crayons, and oil pastels.

Procedure: Instruct clients to place their hands on a sheet of paper and outline them. Next ask group members to fill the outlines in with color and design. Have them cut out the hand outlines and place them within the outsized mandala so that all hands are touching. Ask participants to work together to title the mandala, and create a background if agreed upon by all participants.

Discussion: Discussion focuses on reactions to the completed mandala, and the similarities and differences of the individual hand designs. Celebrating each individual's uniqueness may be explored. Discuss the benefits of making connections and working together as a community.

Figure 78

Two female and three male clients worked on this mandala. Three of the participants had a diagnosis of bipolar disorder; they all suffered from delusional thinking at times. One client was challenged with schizophrenia. Everyone's thinking was clear during this session, except for one man named Larry who appeared tangential and acted very silly at times (rhyming words and reciting phrases from Shakespeare that didn't connect with the group discussion). Larry's contribution was the top, center blue hand with the sequins covering it. He stated he wanted to "have jewels and be king." He haphazardly placed the sequins on his hand, and also cut it out in a rough careless manner. He was pleased with its placement; he liked to be "center stage." Larry remarked that he was glad to be surrounded by the other hands (people) because he liked having company and being with others. He hated being alone and often attended church just to socialize with church members after services.

Hillary painted the red and pink outlined hand (to the left of Larry's hand). She was concerned that she was being too ostentatious by painting her hand totally in red and then outlining it in pink. She asked group members if she was out of line. Hillary seemed relieved when her peers told her they liked her work and found her contribution to be very attractive. She related the red hand to feeling well and to being fashionable. Her niece had recently given her a new wardrobe, which she loved and felt attractive wearing. She also had a new, shorter, stylish haircut, which greatly increased her self-esteem.

A schizophrenic individual named Charlie, who usually kept to himself, created the red hand situated near (just touching) Hillary's hand. Charlie often hallucinated and didn't socialize much unless prompted to do so. Today he was feeling brighter and more social, and represented his positive mood by using red. He was comfortable when Hillary touched her hand to his symbolically in the mandala. At times it was difficult to encourage Charlie to reach out physically, verbally, and/or symbolically, so this was a positive step for him.

The blue hand (next to Charlie's hand) was designed by a middle-aged man named Isaac. Isaac placed glitter on it to represent his excitement about his favorite sports team. He stated that watching football was his passion and helped him cope with stress and loneliness. Talking about sports was also his way of reaching out and communicating with others.

The yellow hand was created by a woman named Crystal who was on her way to recovering from depression. She was meticulous about her appearance and took great care to paint her hand in neatly, even adding nail polish and a large stone ring. When asked about the ring, she stated she deserves some jewels.

After the clients glued the hands they were asked to create a background that also represented connections. They took turns adding symbols, some of which include: hearts, leaves, a peace sign, beads, and the word "love." Group participants shared that they were very pleased with the outcome of the mandala and asked that it be hung up in the art room. They decided to title the work "I Want to Hold Your Hand." They laughed and Larry began singing the old Beatles song. He made up his own words to most of the song.

Two person mandala II

Materials: Drawing paper, markers, crayons, and oil pastels.

Procedure: Clients divide in pairs and work together to create a mandala. They decide whether or not there will be a theme, whether the mandala will be abstract or realistic, and whether there will be specific figures, animals, or items in the design.

Discussion/goals: Discussion focuses on the symbolism depicted in the artwork, each pair's ability to work together, and the ease or difficulty of sharing thoughts and ideas. Examine reactions to the finished product and if clients shared the work equally or one person took a leadership role. Goals include socialization, problem solving, and exploring relationships.

Support mandala

Materials: Drawing paper, markers, crayons, oil pastels, magazines, glue, and scissors.

Procedure: Each participant is given the name of one group member and asked to create a mandala that represents a supportive message for him through images, symbols, design, and words if desired. Clients may mix media.

Discussion: The artist shares his mandala and gives it to the intended recipient. The artist and recipient explore feelings and associations to it. Self-esteem and a feeling of belonging and camaraderie are focused upon.

The group

Materials: Drawing paper, markers, crayons, oil pastels, magazines, glue, and scissors.

Procedure: Each participant is asked to create a mandala representing his feelings about the group, with a focus on his role as group member.

Discussion: Explore the significance of the mandalas and each person's thoughts about his position and importance in the group. Examine the messages relayed through the artwork. Discuss who feels important and who feels inconsequential. Explore how one's role in the group may relate to his role with friends, co-workers, and family members. Self-esteem is explored.

Mandala painting pass[2]

Materials: Circular outlines approximately 18″ to 20″ (46–50cm) in diameter, acrylic paints, and brushes, water.

Procedure: Each client chooses one paint color to work with; he will use *this color only* during the entire session. Clients may mix paints to create shades of one color. For instance, someone may use green and another person may mix green and white to create a mint green. Clients are instructed to take turns adding a design, image, or figure to the circle. They may add words if they please. The mandala continues to develop as each person takes his turn; this occurs until everyone decides the mandala is complete. Ideally it should go around the room at least three times (three turns per person).

Discussion: When it is completed clients may title the artwork, and then discuss their reaction to it, and ask questions of others (if they are comfortable doing so) while observing colors, shapes, and symbols.

Questions to ponder include:

- How does the mandala reflect at least one personality characteristic of each participant?

- How did you feel about participating? For instance, were you comfortable, hesitant, etc.?

- What is your reaction to the placement of the symbols you contributed to the mandala?

- Do any of the symbols stand out or catch your attention? For what reason?

- How does the mandala reflect the mood of group members?

- Does it reflect group unity? What connections, if any, do you notice?

Figure 79

A group of nine individuals, diagnosed with either bipolar disorder, depression and/or co-occurring disorder, worked together to create this mural. It was a diverse group in diagnosis, age, and culture. Some of the clients hadn't met each other before this session. Even before the session formally began, as clients were entering the room, there were some heated discussions concerning patriotism and politics, so it was important to diffuse the anger and work towards cohesiveness and resolution.

Clients were directed to choose one paint color, and, as the mandala was passed from person to person, they were asked to add a symbol or figure. Soothing music was playing in the background. Group members appeared very willing to work and immediately began painting without hesitation. They all worked a few minutes at a time; no one monopolized the mandala or took too long making decisions about what to paint. The group members had been having difficulties verbally being patient with each other, but artistically everyone was polite and considerate. The mandala went around the room three times and everyone carefully added a design. When it was completed clients mentioned that they enjoyed working on it; they felt comfortable and relaxed. One individual stated "I needed to do this; there was no pressure."

The young woman who painted the green area on the bottom middle of the mandala was upset because she felt she ruined the design. She stated she made a mistake and then went over it with the green paint and made a mess. Finally, with support, she decided to transform the blob into a mountain with a tree growing on top of it. Group members supported her for doing this and complimented her work. She smiled but still seemed uncertain, apologizing a number of times until group members pleaded with her to stop apologizing.

Clients seemed to like the large, red infinity sign as well as the peach peace sign. One client was pleased that a woman painted a blue heart near his black crosses (upper left part of mandala). He asked her if she purposely painted her heart there and she responded that she felt a connection to the crosses; he smiled. One man noticed the blue curlicues near the green mountain. He stated that they reminded him of "mini-whirlwinds." Most participants commented on at least one figure; many of them shared their associations to a variety of the symbols.

This project clearly unified the group and calmed group members. Almost everyone seemed relaxed and satisfied when the session was over. The tension had dissipated.

Group mandala II[3]

Materials: The group leader brings a bag filled with small non-fragile objects that the group members may choose from. Objects may include everyday items such as small stuffed animals, Band-Aids, hats, gloves, pillows, memo pads, or even food such as a wrapped candy bar or an apple. Objects from nature such as dried flowers, shells, or small stones may be used. Each group member selects one object, or an object from nature, to represent himself.

Procedure:

1. Group members stand in a circle creating a "Mandala in Motion."

2. Participants choose one of the objects from the bag.

3. Each person is represented by the object they choose from the bag; objects are then "cast" like dice, making sure everyone is at a safe distance.

4. Each person then shares how he feels about the position in which his object has landed (uses psychoanalytic technique of "projection").

5. One-by-one go around in a circle and have each person move his object to a new position, explaining to the group why it feels more comfortable for his object to be in this different place.

6. Through various rounds, participants get to modify/adjust the position of their object until each individual is satisfied with where they sit in relation to the other objects (group members). Participants share reasons they are or aren't satisfied with the position of their object.

7. Continue until everyone is pleased with where his object is situated.

8. Group sizes of approximately 7 to 9 are ideal, but can be done with as few as 5 or as many as 12 individuals.

Discussion: "Allows symbolic exploration of group structure and dynamics, revealing personal feelings towards others. Logistically, a simple activity; facilitation-wise, a potentially difficult and challenging activity; lots of potential for subtle and deep group work" (Loynes 1997). Explore the completed mandala and clients' reactions to it. Encourage participants to share their associations to their chosen object, and feelings about the placement of the other objects in relation to theirs.

Coloring with scarves

Materials: A variety of colorful scarves and a large piece of paper that will cover the floor in front of clients.

Procedure: Group members are told that they will create a mandala using the scarves by placing them on the floor in such a way that a design is created.

Participants form a circle and then choose one scarf. One-by-one each participant places his scarf within the circle. Eventually the scarves will create a design.

After the first round ask clients if they want to keep their scarf where it is or move it.

Each participant has a chance to change its position. After everyone is satisfied with the placement of his scarf and with the mandala as a whole, it is considered completed and group discussion begins.

Discussion: Participants examine the composition, colors, and flow of the mandala.

Group members share their contribution and thoughts about the placement of their scarf. Explore whether the placement relates to the way clients engage in relationships and connects with others, e.g. is the scarf in the middle of the mandala, on the end, near other scarves or isolated?

Hugs mandala[4]

Materials: Drawing paper, markers, crayons, and oil pastels.

Procedure: Ask clients to give imaginary hugs to each other by saying, "I hug you because…" and completing the statement. Have each individual share until everyone receives a hug. After all group members are hugged, have clients create a mandala of their reactions to being hugged or to giving a hug.

Discussion/goals: Discussion focuses on giving and receiving support. Goals include increasing self-esteem, and gaining a greater awareness of strengths and positive characteristics.

Puzzle mandala

Materials: Thin cardboard, markers, crayons, envelopes, oil pastels, colored pencils, pencils, and scissors.

Procedure: Clients outline a circle on the cardboard and cut it out. Then they use a pencil to create standard-looking puzzle piece outlines within the circle. Sample puzzle pieces may be distributed as templates. Next clients draw over the pencil outlines with black marker and then create a design encompassing the entire mandala. It will be suggested that they draw within the puzzle outlines. Lastly, clients cut out the individual puzzle pieces and put them in an envelope. They exchange envelopes so that each person is putting together another person's mandala. When the mandala puzzles are solved they may be glued onto a piece of cardboard or construction paper.

Discussion: Clients focus on problem solving, abstract thinking, and sharing. Discussion centers on the ease or difficulty of solving the puzzle, the appearance and associations to the mandala, and the connections made by working together.

Notes

1 Project directed by Tracylynn Navarro MA, ATR-BC. Ms. Navarro described the project and its goals.

 Another variation of this mural is to have clients draw individual mandalas, cut them out and glue or tape them to a large sheet of mural paper. They may draw an environment around their mandala or create an environment for all of the mandalas (the group can decide how to proceed).

2 The diameter depends on the number of clients attending the session.

3 Description of a Group Dynamics Exercise, from Chris Loynes' exercise from the Tenth National Outdoor Education Conference, 1997, in Perth, Western Australia. It is based on an idea from Roger Greenaway. This directive has been modified slightly to suit the needs of the client; it was originally designed as a teaching exercise for graduate students. In the original directive the participants bring their own objects to share.

4 Based on an idea by Evelyn Sutkowski, LPC, LCADC.

Chapter 6

Stress Reduction

Mandalas specifically aimed at stress reduction help clients to relax, reduce anxiety, lessen the degree and frequency of anxiety attacks, and learn how to be mindful. Clients acquire skills to cope with illness, fear, frustration, and relationship problems. They discover the importance of positive thinking, self-processing, and self-talk. Clients become skilled in identifying and changing erroneous thinking such as catastrophizing, over-generalizing, and labeling. They learn methods to stop worrying such as thought stopping, positive self-talk, and identifying realistic and unrealistic fears. They practice meditation techniques such as deep breathing and guided imagery. Meditation helps individuals find a sense of calm, inner peace, and balance. Some research shows that meditation techniques may improve immune system functioning, allergies, asthma, cancer, depression, fatigue, heart disease, sleep problems, and high blood pressure. Mandala work helps clients understand the importance of being mindful. Mindfulness increases self-esteem, self-awareness, and self-acceptance. It improves concentration and creativity. When clients are in the "here and now," they have more physical stamina; they are more confident and their moods are more even; they have better ability to concentrate and memory improves.

Clients become increasingly aware of harmful roles they may take on, such as being a victim or scapegoat in the family. They identify negative relationships and life patterns, and try to change and/or improve them. Creating and analyzing their mandalas helps clients learn coping techniques such as choosing one's battles and focusing on the positive aspects of their life instead of the negative. They discover how to be patient by taking one day at a time, taking tiny steps forward and not allowing themselves to be overwhelmed by adversity. Clients learn how to identify and avoid anxiety triggers. They focus on support systems and asking for help when needed. Individuals come to understand the importance that attitude and motivation play in reducing stress, and they learn self-soothing techniques such as taking long walks, celebrating achievements, and exercising. Clients learn to take care of themselves physically and psychologically and to focus on their strengths and attributes.

Mandala mindfulness exercise

Materials: Drawing paper, paper plates, pastels, crayons, and markers.

Procedure: Ask patients to close their eyes, relax, and listen to the sounds around them (birds chirping, sounds from the heater or air conditioner, wind blowing, etc.). Ask them to just focus on the sounds and let all other thoughts float away. After a few minutes suggest that they outline a circle and draw what they experienced within the circle. They may use color and shape, or objects and figures, to represent their thoughts and feelings.

Discussion/goals: Discussion focuses on the importance of becoming mindful in one's life. The importance of taking time to stop and smell the roses, not dwelling on the past or worrying about the future may be explored. Goals include stress reduction and relaxation.

Peaceful mind mandala

Materials: Drawing paper, markers, oil pastels, and crayons.

Procedure: Clients symbolize their mind at rest. Have participants depict the calmness and peacefulness associated with being mindful within their mandala.

Discussion: Explore the colors, symbols, shapes, and images of serenity. Explore ways to relax and reduce anxiety.

Stress

Materials: Drawing paper, markers, oil pastels, and crayons.

Procedure: Clients write the word "stress" in the center of the circle in "doodle format." They may create the word out of doodles or place doodles within the letters that compose the word "stress." Next instruct participants to symbolize what it feels like to be anxious by drawing images, symbols, colors, and shapes surrounding the word "stress."

Discussion: Clients share the colors and images of stress. They relate the artwork to bodily feelings and disturbing thoughts. Methods to deal with tension and discomfort are explored.

Healthy life style

Materials: Sketches of symbols and cartoons representing health, and photos of people engaged in activities that promote wellness. Provide glue, scissors, pencils, pens, oil pastels, and markers.

Procedure: Go to "Google Images" on the computer and click "Images for a Healthy Lifestyle." There you will see a variety of pictures representing healthy living. There you will see a variety of pictures representing healthy living. Print about 30 different photos, trying to place 4–6 on each page. Distribute the photos pages to group members so they have a broad choice from which to choose. Suggest clients cut out the pictures that appeal to them, and place them within the mandala to create a collage. They may add their own artwork and associated words if desired.

Discussion: Explore how to lead a healthy life style by examining and reflecting on the chosen photos. Ask clients if their mandalas symbolize what they are presently doing to heal themselves. Discuss ways to improve nutrition and overall fitness.

Stress release and pastels

Materials: Drawing paper, soothing music, and pastels.

Procedure: Play mellow music and ask clients to lightly spread the pastels within the mandala outline. They may sway gently as they do this. Encourage participants to let their fingers take them wherever they please within the circular shape. Tell them not to think of a design or theme; they should just move freely and create an image to the music.

Discussion: Discussion focuses on the feelings experienced while spreading the pastels on the paper. Usually group members feel peaceful and carefree while designing with the pastels. Ask group participants to discuss their stress level while doing this exercise. Explore who felt relaxed and who felt anxious.

Black/white mandala meditation[1]

Materials: Black pastel paper and white pencils.

Procedure: Same procedure as the 'Black/white mandalas' on pp.95–96.

According to Raja Yoga and Hindu philosophy, this work of bringing in the light builds up an etheric or astral blueprint of energy in and around the body, which strengthens with each practice. This blueprint will eventually affect the physical body and this is why mandalas or sacred symbols are often used to promote healing.

Carl Jung writes: "When I began drawing the mandalas, I saw that everything, all paths I had been following all the steps I had taken were leading back to a single point—namely, to the midpoint. It became increasingly plain to me that the mandala is the centre. It is the exponent of all paths. It is the path to the centre, to individuation" (Jung and Jaffée 1989, p.196).

Discussion: Same discussion as the 'Black/white mandalas' on p.96.

The Sun

Materials: Drawing paper, markers, pastels, oil pastels, and crayons.

Procedure: Ask clients to outline a circle from a paper plate. Now suggest they close their eyes and imagine that a large bright sun is emitting its rays down on them. Ask them to think about the warmth and feel of the rays. Suggest that the rays are penetrating all body parts: their head, face, neck, shoulders, back, arms, stomach, legs, feet, and toes. Ask group members to feel the healing warmth and soothing comfort the sun provides. Next suggest clients fill in the circle with symbols and designs representing a sensation of healing, their body as it becomes healthier, and/or the sun emitting its rays.

Discussion: Examine the verbal and creative responses to the imagery. Discuss how positive thinking and "warm" feelings affect the body and mind. Explore ways clients can nurture themselves.

Relax and express

Materials: Relaxing music, drawing paper, markers, and pastels.

Procedure: Instruct clients to outline a circle from a paper plate, and then ask them to close their eyes, relax, and listen mindfully to the CD by Tracy Carreon, *A Moment's Peace* #7: "Garden of the Soul." Encourage clients to focus on all aspects of the music while they listen. Then ask them to fill in the mandala with what they felt and/ or imagined while they listened to the CD.

Discussion/goals: Discussion focuses on the connection between the artwork created and the music. Goals include increased relaxation, exploration of stress reduction techniques and feelings associated with being tranquil.

The wave

Materials: Drawing paper, pastels, crayons, and markers.

Procedure: Ask patients to visualize themselves riding a wave at the beach. Suggest they visualize the size of the wave, the speed and color of the wave, the strength of the wave, and how they are feeling emotionally and physically. Ask them to visualize the way in which they are riding the wave (for instance, are they on a surfboard, are they actually in the wave, under the wave, etc.) Ask them about the water (is it cold, warm, hard, soft, comforting, or threatening). Then ask them to draw this visual experience using the circle as their canvas.

Discussion/goals: The wave may be used to represent how the client approaches issues, problems, and challenges. Discussion focuses on how the client rides the wave; does he glide on top of it, dive into it, or fall under the water? Explore how the wave can represent life's challenges, and discuss what specific challenges group members are experiencing. Examine methods to ride "life's waves," e.g. "When hungry can you ride the wave of hunger and wait until dinner to eat, or do you need to eat that cookie right now? When stressed can you take deep breaths, do relaxation exercises and allow the stress to decrease and/or pass?" Goals include identifying, changing, and developing new coping strategies.

The Five Senses

Materials: Drawing paper, pastels, crayons, markers, variety of objects such as the examples below, and basket or box.

Procedure: Fill a basket or box with a variety of objects, each of which should clearly represent all of the senses. An example would be a ridged potato chip. It has a distinct smell, you can feel the ridges, it has a salty taste, and it appears oval and somewhat wavy in design. It has a pale yellow color. If you break it in half you can hear a snap. Another example would be a dough ball. It is pale beige, it feels soft and squishy, it also sounds squishy when you squeeze it, it tastes doughy, and it has a distinctive smell. Ask each client to choose one of the objects and examine it for a few minutes. Then direct each individual to explore his object one sense at a time. After this is completed suggest that group members outline a circle with a template and draw the object they chose within the circle using color and shape. Suggest that they keep in mind the feelings they experienced during the exercise.

Discussion/goals: Each group member is given the opportunity to voice his thoughts about the exercise. They may be asked to share which sense they focused upon most and the reasons for their choice. Feelings and thoughts about centering on one object may be examined. Goals include learning how to be in the moment, how to let extraneous thoughts pass by, and how to focus on one thing at a time in order to decrease stress and lessen troublesome thoughts.

Body scan

Materials: Drawing paper, pastels, crayons, and markers.

Procedure: Lead group members in a full body scan. Have them close their eyes (if they are comfortable doing so) and suggest they relax their eyebrows, eyes, nose, mouth, jaw, neck, shoulders, arms, hands, chest, stomach, thighs, legs, feet, and toes. Go through each body part slowly and in a soft, low voice. Soothing music may be playing as you do this. After the exercise ask group members to draw a line through the mandala separating it in half. Suggest they draw how their body felt before the exercise, on one side of the mandala, and how their body felt after the exercise, on the other side of it.

Discussion/goals: Discussion may focus on how the artwork reflects the relaxation experience and the changes that occurred during the exercise. Goals include learning how to self soothe and de-stress in order to attain a peaceful state of being and to help ward off anxiety and panic attacks.

Release

Materials: Relaxing music, drawing paper, pastels, crayons, and markers.

Procedure: Play soothing background music. Ask clients to relax and pay attention to their breath. Ask them to spend a few minutes breathing in and out slowly. If they feel comfortable have them close their eyes. Suggest that clients visualize what they are breathing out. Ask them to think about size, shape, color, and texture. Next ask them to outline a circle using a template and draw "what they breathed out" within the circle. Examples may include breathing out stress, anger, fear, etc. They may use any type of design to depict their thoughts.

Discussion/goals: Discussion focuses on the relaxation experience, the feeling of release when breathing out, and the emotions/feelings depicted in the artwork. Clients have the opportunity to gain a better understanding of their feelings by analyzing and observing the size, color, and design of their mandala. Goals include release of negative feelings and stress.

Loving breath

Materials: Drawing paper, pastels, crayons, and markers.

Procedure: Suggest that clients slowly breathe in and out, and imagine their breath is embracing them. Explain that they are being "bathed in peace, love and warmth." Suggest they breathe in beauty and calmness, and breathe out comfort and solace. After participating in this exercise ask clients to draw themselves being embraced by something or someone they love. Have clients use the circular outline to help them feel focused and soothed.

Discussion/goals: Discussion focuses on how clients felt during the exercise, and the way they designed their drawing. Encourage them to share how it feels to be embraced, and explore who or what embraced them in their mandala. Goals include exploration of ways to achieve inner peace and feelings of comfort.

Ocean mandala: A relaxation exercise

Materials: Drawing paper, markers, oil pastels, pastels, and crayons.

Procedure: Have clients share reasons they like to go to the seashore. Then ask them to draw their interpretation of the seashore including items or things that make them feel relaxed. Suggest to clients this is a stress-reducing exercise; they may want to visualize themselves relaxing on the sand, on the boardwalk, or in the water while they draw. They may use pastels to gently spread the color and represent the feeling of the seashore. Soothing background music may be played as an additional stress reducer.

Discussion/goals: Discussion focuses on the feelings elicited while drawing and the symbolism portrayed. Goals include stress reduction, focusing on positive imagery, and self-soothing.

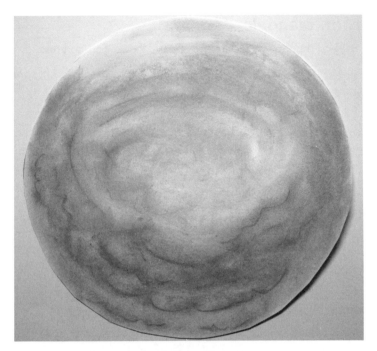

Figure 80

A woman in her 60s, named Pearl, used pastels to design this calming mandala. She stated she thought of cool ocean breezes, and gentle waves. She pictured the sun setting and the temperature getting a little cooler. Pearl visualized quietness and peace. She remarked she could smell the salty ocean air and was even able to imagine she heard seagulls in the background. She shared that she could almost feel the soft, warm sand under her blanket as she lay on the beach. Pearl spoke about visits to the shore with her family, especially when her children were young. She recounted an incident where her children made a hole in the sand so deep her husband went in it and was almost completely hidden. The children filled a pail with water and poured it on his head. The children laughed hysterically and so did she. She remarked that she was happiest during that period of her life.

Tension mandala

Materials: Drawing paper, markers, oil pastels, and crayons.

Procedure: Ask clients to close their eyes and breathe deeply. Suggest that they listen to their bodies for a few minutes (they may listen to their heart beating, stomach grumbling, the sound of their breathing, etc.). Ask them to focus on how they feel (are they comfortable, are they experiencing any aches, any tension in their body?). Encourage them to draw any tension or any stiffness they feel.

Discussion/goals: Discussion focuses on where the tension is and methods of decreasing the stress and discomfort. Goals include self-awareness and exploring coping skills.

White on black mandalas: Inner light[2]

Materials: Black pastel paper, white pencil.

Procedure: Have clients relax and listen to calming music for a short period of time. Suggest they focus on their strengths, passion, faith, unique characteristics, and the love they have to give to themselves and others. Next ask participants to use the white pencil on the black paper to portray their "inner light" (beliefs, conscience, divine presence) within the mandala.

Discussion: Explore the importance and distinctiveness of each individual. Examine the energy represented by the white shapes, forms, and lines that create the mandala. Discuss the healing energy that people possess and can utilize when they are feeling ill emotionally and physically.

Stress mandala

Materials: Drawing paper, pastels, crayons, markers.

Procedure: Direct clients to draw things that stress them. Suggest that they may include people, places, and other physical and emotional stressors in their life. It would be beneficial if clients included at least two stressors in their artwork.

Discussion/goals: Discussion focuses on the way in which the stressors are depicted, the type of stressors, their size, shape, etc. The artwork allows clients to view and measure their stressors in terms of significance and achievability by observing many of these factors.

The circular mandala serves as a safe structure from which to explore uncomfortable issues and feelings. Goals include examining challenges and exploring coping mechanisms.

Wind, tree, sky

Materials: Soothing music, drawing paper, markers, oil pastels, crayons, and paper plates.

Procedure: Play soft, soothing music and take participants through a brief guided imagery. Encourage group members to close their eyes and sit in a relaxed position, and imagine they are sitting in a comfortable chair, enjoying a warm, beautiful summer day.

The birds are singing and there is calming stillness. The comforting sound of flowing water is heard from a nearby stream and the sound of leaves rustling in the wind is like music to the ears. The air smells fresh and sweet. Breathing it in cleanses one's soul.

The branches and leaves on the trees are gently swaying in the breeze. A small brown squirrel is scurrying up one of the branches. A cardinal with a bright red breast is perched high on an evergreen. All is well in the world. The sun is warm, but not too hot. It is sending healing rays that penetrate your body. You can feel the warmth in your face, chest, arms, and legs. The healing warmth is flowing through your veins and into your blood stream. It is making you healthy, vital, and strong. You feel one with nature and you are at peace.

Keep the music playing and allow clients to contemplate the imagery for a few minutes. Then ask them to create a mandala that represents the feelings they experienced. Have them include at least one tree, and a representation of the wind and sky in the mandala.

Discussion: Explore the peacefulness attained during the guided imagery and while designing the mandala. Examine ways to experience serenity at home. Discuss how participants relate to the key symbols (tree, sky, and wind) and to the power and beauty of nature.

A safe place

Materials: Drawing paper, markers, crayons, and oil pastels.

Procedure: Clients are asked to draw a place they feel sheltered and secure.

Discussion: Clients discuss the benefits they derive from their safe place. They are encouraged to use their sanctuary as a way to build strength, and to lessen anxiety by thinking about it when they are tense. Explore how the shape of the circle can add to the soothing feeling elicited. Relaxation techniques which focus on visual imaging of the sanctuary may be explored. For example, individuals may be asked to close their eyes, take a few deep breaths and visualize their safe place focusing on colors, smells, and sounds, and positive feelings.

Notes

1   www.heavenearthhealing.com, accessed July 13, 2012.

2   Inner light mandala is modified from www.heavenearthhealing.com, Robert and Shauna Kendall.

Chapter 7

Mixed Media Mandala

The use of mixed media allows clients the chance to experiment with various materials and learn how to combine an assortment of items to create a specific project or design. Individuals learn to build and put things together, to problem solve, and to be resourceful. They test out supplies and try different ways of connecting objects. Recycling is often focused upon.

A wide variety of creative materials fall under this category. Some include using decorative items such as beads and glitter, shells, buttons, stones, recycled materials such as plastic bags and old CDs, and leaves, flowers, and acorns. Clay of various sorts, nuts and bolts, and wooden pieces may be utilized. Working with these materials enables clients to learn to view things three dimensionally. Clients may observe their artwork from more than one vantage point; they learn to look at it from all angles and directions. A new dimension is added to the mandala work, which generally takes more thought and problem solving. This enhances abstract thinking. Ideally this thinking becomes generalized and helps the client better understand and view his problems, concerns, and relationships in a broader, healthier, and more realistic manner. It helps diminish black and white thinking. Following directions, organizing media, and working on projects from start to completion enhances focusing and helps clients derive a sense of accomplishment. Individuals gain greater control and self-esteem as they learn how to problem solve and accept creative challenges.

Tie dye mandala[1]

Materials: Baby wipes, rubber bands, watercolor markers, plastic gloves, and drawing paper.

Procedure:

1. Pass out the baby wipes, one per client.

2. Next distribute about four rubber bands each.

3. Participants will tie the bands very tightly around different sections of the baby wipe. They can roll their baby wipe or fold it different ways before they tie them.

4. Suggest clients put the gloves on and then place the baby wipe on drawing paper and color between the rubber bands with the different color markers. Make sure participants press the markers into the wipe so the ink will go all the way through.

5. Next clients cut the rubber bands off and a beautiful mandala design is created. The wipe can be glued on a sheet of drawing paper or construction paper when dried. If the design doesn't turn out to be circular the client can place a paper plate over the design, trace a circle, and then cut it out.

Discussion: Explore reactions to the creative process and the overall design of the mandala. Examine the unique details, colors, and shapes of each creation. Encourage clients to share ways in which the mandala reflects personality characteristics.

Clay mandala[2]

Materials: Many types of clay work well for this project. Other materials needed include a rolling pin, water or spray bottle, waxed paper, a round cookie cutter, popsicle sticks, shells, beads, stampers, buttons, beads, small wood pieces, sequins, pipe cleaners, and any items that can be pushed into the clay to leave an impression.

Procedure: "A different approach to mandala making." Introduce mandalas (circles used for focusing and healing) to the group. Discuss the aspects of a circular pattern, wholeness, unity, etc.

1. Clients are asked to experiment with the clay by molding, kneading, and manipulating it.

2. Demonstrate how to create a flat circular cutout from the clay on a square of waxed paper: wedge clay and then roll it out using a rolling pin to ½″ (1cm) in thickness.

3. Depress the round cookie cutter into the clay.

4. Remove excess and save in a plastic bag.

5. Once each client has a clay circle, they can choose how they would like to complete their mandala using other materials provided.

Discussion/goals: Ask clients to share how they felt creating the mandala and have them describe their design and/or pattern. Suggest they share the meaning of their work. Discuss whether there are any themes common among members of the group? Question how the creation of the mandala relates to focusing inward, and/or wholeness? Goals include self-awareness, focusing, and expression of mood and feeling.

Stone mosaic mandala

Materials: Small colorful rocks and stones, strong glue or glue gun, and cardboard.

Procedure: Instruct clients to trace a circle from a template onto the cardboard. Suggest they create a design utilizing the stones, gluing them onto the mandala one by one until an appealing design is formed.

Discussion/goals: Discussion focuses on the colors, shine, texture, and placement of the stones, and the client's reaction to the finished product. Goals include increased self-esteem, problem solving, and stress reduction.

Mandala bottle cap jewelry[3]

Materials: Tops from water bottles, permanent markers that won't smudge on plastic, sharp small scissors or tiny sharp screwdriver, string, cord, wool, or thin ribbon.

Procedure: Everyone collects bottle caps until there is one for each group member. The group facilitator pokes holes through the top and bottom of the caps with small sharp scissors or any other sharp instrument. The cap will be in an upright position when this is done.

Clients are instructed to decorate the cap in any way they please. A small bead should be put through a long straight pin in order to create a more stable and attractive base for the focal point (the cap). The straight pin should have a small metal base so that the bead is able to stay on it, and not slip through the pin and onto the floor. The top of the pin will stick out of the bottle cap. It is bent, and a loop will be created with the remainder of it. String, yarn, ribbon, etc. is placed through the loop and a personal necklace is created.

Discussion/goals: Discussion focuses on the necklace designs and the client's reactions to his creative work. Explore whether or not the artwork is self-representative. Goals include focusing, problem solving, following step-by-step directions, the increase in self-esteem that comes about by working on a project from start to finish and then having a finished product to wear, share, or give to someone special.

Memories

Materials: 8˝ (20cm) diameter doilies (or larger), pastels, crayons, and markers. The circular doilies will serve as the mandala.

Procedure: Ask clients to fill the doily in with a beautiful memory. The lovely, intricate design of the doily lends itself to thoughts about births, marriages, and other special occasions.

Discussion/goals: Discussion focuses on joyful experiences and wonderful thoughts about the past. Clients are encouraged to focus on the positive and explore methods to attain happiness and fulfillment in their lives.

Autumn/Halloween mandala

Materials: Paint, markers, permanent black markers, magazines, glue, and scissors.

Procedure: Suggest clients paint their mandalas with autumn-like colors such as orange, golden yellow, or light brown. After the mandalas dry have group members add Halloween and/or autumnal symbols such as candy corn, candy apples, scarecrows, colorful leaves, a Jack-o-lantern, etc. Participants may use markers, paints, and/or photos from magazines to decorate the mandalas.

Discussion: Encourage group members to share the significance of the images and symbols that compose the mandalas. Support clients to reminisce about past autumns, e.g. Did they go trick-or-treating? Did they pick apples in an orchard? Did they make apple cider or candy apples at home? Explore reactions to the colder weather and change of seasons.

Vegetable/fruit mandala

Materials: Slices/pieces of vegetables and fruits such as figs, grass stalks, raisins, grapefruit and orange peels, bay leaves, carrot slices, lettuce and spinach pieces, bay leaves, tomatoes, cabbage, glue, scissors, markers, oil pastels, and crayons.

Procedure: Fill in the circle with the fruit and vegetables (cut and trim them to help create a pleasing composition); add color with markers or oil pastels to complete the design if desired.

Discussion: Explore the beauty and unique characteristics of the fruit and vegetables. Examine how the mandala relates to one's personality and life style. Discuss how people "feed themselves" (give themselves support and nurturance).

Fabric scraps mandala

Materials: Strong glue, a variety of fabric scraps, and scissors.

Procedure: Provide a large selection of colorful fabric scraps. Suggest that group members use them to compose a design within the mandala.

Discussion: Encourage clients to observe patterns, colors, and images that may appear. Discuss the texture of the fabric and the placement of the materials. Support group members to associate the mandalas to clothing they have sewn, worn, or bought for themselves or others over the years. Discuss the impact fabric has on our lives, how what we wear often reflects aspects of our personalities. Ask clients to share their thoughts on this topic and to share how one article of clothing they are wearing reflects something about their character.

Feather mandala

Materials: A variety of feathers, markers, scissors, glue, sequins, and glitter.

Procedure: Share that to Native American Indians "feathers represent ascension and spiritual strength. Feathers were worn by Chiefs to symbolize their communication with Spirit, and to express their celestial wisdom."[4] Then ask participants to fill in the mandala with an array of feathers and an assortment of small objects such as sequins to create a pleasing design and to represent their own spirit, force, strength, or character.

Discussion: Clients share what spirituality means to them and what they consider their higher power. Explore how the mandalas reflect their strengths and beliefs.

Figure 81

A 58-year-old man named Rob, who was diagnosed with bipolar disorder, was pleased with the outcome of his mandala. He took special care to use all the colors provided and attempted to space them as evenly as possible. He began from the inside out and worked his way around the periphery of the circle. Rob enjoyed this directive; he whistled and sang a variety of silly songs while he worked. He stated that working with feathers was fun and easy. He repeated what the therapist said at the beginning of the session, "You can't be wrong; it's just expressing your feelings." During discussion he shared that the mandala represented "being a warrior. I am a warrior for working so hard to stay well and fighting this illness." Rob remarked that when he played football in college he acted like a warrior, "You had to be tough or they'd pulverize you." He continued, "My father was a warrior in the army; he risked his life to save others, and he died in the war." As the dialogue continued Rob stated that the artwork also represented "being all over the place; I like to spread out." He smiled a lot as group members supported him and complemented his style.

Figure 82

Jarred, a creative man in his late 30s, diagnosed with schizophrenia, chose not to use the feathers, although he experimented with them for a while. Instead he drew a heart with a sword piercing it. Surrounding the heart are "leaves." According to Jarred the sword and heart represent "My constant working on my struggles—struggling psychologically." The green leaves represent "peace and my intelligence." When asked, he remarked that the peace and intelligence are his guardian angels, and "sometimes my brother." He shared that his writing (he is writing a novel) "is what keeps me going."

Sugar mandala[5]

Materials: Food coloring, 1–2 cups of sugar, small plastic bag, paper, scissors, paper plate, sponges, and sponge brushes with handles.

Procedure: "Participants create a funnel from a piece of paper by molding the paper so that it appears cone-like. Tape it to stay in place. The smaller the funnel hole, the easier it will be to manipulate the sugar. One drop of food coloring is placed in a plastic bag with 1–2 cups of sugar. Then the bag is kneaded so the sugar gets colored evenly." More coloring may be added if the tint is not rich enough. Pour the sugar in the funnel and tip it a little so the sugar pours out very slowly. A sponge brush or thin paintbrush may also be used to create thinner lines. Instruct participants to create a realistic or abstract image. "When the design is completed, discuss, admire, and then pour the sugar back into the bag. This is a non-permanent piece of art."

Discussion: Explore the reality that nothing is lasting; change is part of our lives. Discuss the significance of traditional sand mandalas, which are "swept back to earth after they are created to emphasize the impermanence of life." Explore clients' thoughts and associations to their mandalas, and their reactions to the transience of the artwork.

Personal objects mandala[6]

Materials: Balsa wood circle approximately the size of a large plate or circular piece of cardboard, glue gun or very strong glue such as wood glue, paint, brushes, items that are self-representative and that tell a story, such as photos, old jewelry, souvenirs from vacations and special days, signs, labels, and ticket stubs, etc.

Procedure: The group leader provides everyone with a wooden or cardboard circle. Participants paint their circle and let it dry. Then clients decide how to place their chosen objects, and glue them one by one until a design is formed.

Discussion: Clients share the items incorporated into the design and the significance of the artwork. They discuss ways in which the mandala represents portions of their life and experiences.

Shell mandala

Materials: A variety of shells, glue gun or strong glue, paint, and brushes.

Procedure: Clients are asked to paint their mandala a calming color, perhaps a color that reminds them of the ocean. Next ask them to select a variety of shells and fill in the circle with the shells so that an image of the seashore is created.

Discussion: Participants share associations to the shells and the overall collage. Visits to the beach and previous summer vacations may be explored. Discuss feelings and images evoked by thinking about the seashore, sand, water, seagulls cawing, and the fresh, salty air.

Plastic bag mandala[7]

Materials: A variety of plastic bags (all different colors, patterns, and logos), glue, tape, pencils, paper plates, and scissors.

Procedure: According to Ms. Fleck: "The simplest way to explain my process is to say that I cut the plastic bags and then tape the pieces together. The cutting can get very sophisticated. I use many quilt making tools such as rotary cutters, shaped cutting templates, and circle cutters. I also use a beam compass for drawing large circles, various Exacto™ knives and a reducing glass (the opposite of a magnifying glass) for viewing and assessing the large highly patterned mandalas while they are in progress."

In the therapy group clients will utilize scissors, tape, and glue, and glue the pieces of plastic within the circle until a pleasing design is formed.

Discussion: Participants share reactions to working with plastic and explore the positives and negatives of the material. Resourcefulness, creativity, and abstract thinking are focused upon.

Clients share associations to the mandalas, and discuss the ways recycling can be helpful to each individual and to the environment. The idea of making something beautiful from garbage can be related to renewal and recreating oneself and one's life.

Figure 83
Mandala illustrated in the color insert
[This innovative, creative mandala was designed by Virginia Fleck]

Button mandala

Materials: Cardboard, assortment of buttons, strong glue or glue gun, paint, brushes, paper plate, and pencils.

Procedure: Group members paint the circle using energizing colors. When the circle is dry have clients create a button design within the mandala.

Discussion: "Button collecting was recognized as an organized hobby through the founding of the National Button Society in 1938."[8] Buttons for practical purposes have had significance since the thirteenth century; they had been used mostly for adornments or seals previous to the thirteenth century.

Encourage clients to share their mandalas and examine the significance of their button-laden designs. Have them point out particularly attractive or unusual buttons. Explore images or thoughts elicited when working with the buttons. For instance: Do the buttons bring up memories such as learning how to button a blouse, or having difficulty unbuttoning a shirt? Ask clients, "Have you sewed buttons on any item of clothing or do you remember a family member sewing for you?" Explore how buttons relate to the themes of necessity, modesty, style, relationships, and "buttoning up" (not talking).

Soul mandala

Materials: Drawing paper, markers, oil pastels, crayons, magazine photos, collage materials such as cotton balls and fabric pieces, wool, paints, and brushes.

Procedure: Participants illustrate a representation of their soul (spirit, essence, and core) within the circle using a variety of materials. They may mix materials or use just one type of material.

Discussion: Group members share their essence (who they genuinely are, how they see themselves). Explore what is in their heart and soul. Examine self-esteem, self-awareness, and the uniqueness of each individual.

Figure 84
Mandala illustrated in the color insert

A woman in her 50s named Shara spent about four sessions creating this mandala designed from pre-cut pieces of wool. She deliberately chose colors that "went well together" and were coordinated. She glued one piece on at a time trying to keep the pieces evenly spaced, as close together as possible. Shara remarked that the mandala "looked like her." It was bright, busy and "going around in circles." She shared that she was a complex person with a "good heart." She could be moody but would go out of her way to help a friend. She remarked that at the moment she felt discombobulated but was hoping she'd feel steadier and clearer in the near future. She stated, when asked by other group members, that she was generally content with her personality and self-esteem, and satisfied that her "Karma was positive."

Life cycle mandala[9]

Materials: Rough copy of drawing, and one photocopy of drawing, sharpie marker, clay, rolling pins, canvas, pin tools (to attach or cut clay), fettling knives, tray, damp cloth, plastic bags, variety of clay tools, slip, tempera paint (acrylic paint may also be used as well as underglazes and crystal clear glaze), brushes (variety of sizes), crystal clear acrylic spray paint or alternate, flat black acrylic paint, and prismacolor colored pencils.

Procedure: Clients plan and design a mandala with a nature theme, and then outline the drawing in thin sharpie marker. Photocopy the drawings so clients have a copy to use as a tracer on the clay.

Participants roll out a slab of clay about ½″ (13 mm) thick. Then they use a pre-cut tracer (8″ or 23 cm) to cut out the circle. They transfer the clay slab onto a plastic tray (with paper towel on the bottom so as not to stick) and then lay the photocopy over the clay. They poke holes through the design with a pin tool (sometimes outlining the drawing with a pen will transfer enough, too). Next, they roll out a coil that goes around the edge (and score and slip that in place). From there, they decide which objects they want to build up and which they just want to carve. They use the photocopy as a template to make the different objects stand out. After they are fired they will be painted with tempera paint. Acrylic gloss medium may be applied to give a shiny look.

Discussion: Discuss feelings evoked while viewing the mandala and handling it. Clients examine how the colors, design, texture, and consistency of the clay affect the nature of the mandala (literally and figuratively). Examine the impact nature has on one's life and its importance in mediation and mindfulness.

Coin mandalas

Materials: Cardboard, a variety of coins: real or imitation, such as coins found in children's games, pennies, nickels, and dimes. In addition, paint, brushes, water, heavy-duty glue or glue gun.

Procedure: Clients paint the circle one or more colors. Next they create a pleasing design utilizing the coins, taking care to glue them carefully so they adhere to the circle.

Discussion: Participants discuss their reaction to the construction of the mandalas, and the significance of utilizing coins to create them. Group members explore the value of money and what types of things they need and/or desire in order to feel fulfilled.

Mandala drawing on an old CD[10]

Materials: Old CD, white spray paint, fine tipped black sharpie permanent marker and sharpie colored markers, watery glue, ruler, and pencil.

Procedure:

1. Spray paint the CD until it is totally white.

2. Let it dry and then brush watery glue on it to create a more slippery surface.

3. After the glue dries use a ruler and pencil to estimate lines that would divide the CD into eight equal sections. Have a template available for people who need extra assistance.

4. Using the pencil fill in the first section with simple diamonds, circles, leaves, curves, and other shapes.

5. Repeat the design pattern in the other seven sections until all of the sections match each other.

6. After the pencil designs and lines are drawn, trace them with a fine tip black sharpie marker.

7. Lastly, the shapes are colored in with colorful sharpie markers.

Discussion: Observe and discuss the various patterns created and the colors and shapes utilized. Ask clients to relate the patterns and balance of the design to the way they are balancing their lives. Pose questions such as:

1. Do you think your life is presently in balance? If not, what are the reasons for feeling off balance?

2. Do you notice specific patterns in your daily routine or behaviors?

3. Do you prefer a structured schedule, or a more laid back, "whatever happens, let the day evolve" approach to your daily routine?

Figure 85

Gravel mandala[11]

Materials: Colored gravel, poster board, paper plates, glue such as Elmer's™ glue or any strong glue that can be squeezed from a tube, wax coated or leather, black thin shoelaces, and a pencil.

Procedure:

1. The client outlines a circle on the cardboard with a pencil, using a paper plate as a template.

2. He then uses a pencil to create a design of shapes within the circle, or he might divide the circle into sixths or eighths for a more symmetrical look.

3. The shoelaces are cut the exact size of the perimeter of the circle.

4. Next a thick layer of glue is placed on the perimeter of the circle only.

5. The shoelaces are placed on the glue so that the laces become the circular outline; and the gravel will be placed within this outline.

6. Next each shape is filled in with glue (not outlined with the laces unless desired) and a full layer of various colored gravel is placed on each shape until a design is completed.

7. The mandala should dry for a few hours.

Discussion: Discuss the texture of the mandala and the gravelly feel and appearance. Explore the rough quality, shapes, and colors utilized. Ask participants to share their reactions to the process of creating the mandala, its symbolism and significance as it relates to mood and feeling. Explore whether clients see themselves as "rough" (hardened or difficult to deal with) or "smooth" (mellow, gentle).

Nature mandala collage

Materials: Items from nature such as twigs, pebbles, flowers, grass, acorns, leaves, pine cones, etc.

Procedure: Walk in a park or woodsy area and collect small appealing items that could be glued onto the mandala in order to create a design. Next cut a round piece of cardboard about the size of a plate. Using a hot glue gun or other strong glue, such as

Gorilla Glue™, begin gluing the objects on the mandala in a circular manner until a design is formed.

Discussion: Explore the items utilized and the wonder of nature. Discuss the unity we have with our environment and the calming effect nature has upon us. Explore feelings about the earth, the elements and their effect on our mood, behavior, and well being.

Drawing to music

Materials: Recordings of various melodies, paper, pastels, markers, and mandalas.

Procedure: A lively, somber, and then mellow song may be played. While each song is played clients are encouraged to draw their feelings to the music within the mandala.

Discussion/goals: Discussion focuses on examining feelings and memories evoked by the music. Goals include expression of issues and concerns.

Glitter and shine

Materials: Cardboard, glue, scissors, glitter, sequins, small stones, buttons, etc.

Procedure: Fill in the mandala with glitter of various colors, sequins, shimmering stones, and any other shiny objects.

Discussion: Clients share ways in which they relate to the striking mandala. Have them share ways in which they shine. Explore outstanding achievements and experiences. Ask participants, "What people, places, feelings, things and/or events make you glisten; what puts a twinkle in your eye?"

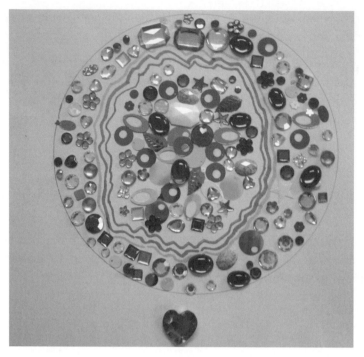

Figure 86

Charla, an attractive and intelligent 39-year-old woman overcoming anxiety and depression, enjoyed designing this dazzling mandala. She took great care to place and then glue the stones and sequins in a specific order. Charla described the creative project as very relaxing and enjoyable. She especially liked working with the tiny colorful flowers because they reminded her of the flowers her husband Jack recently bought her for their tenth anniversary. She stated that Jack is very supportive and devoted, "He is helping me through this ordeal." Charla related the mandala to her "old bubbly personality" and to the question, "What puts a twinkle in your eye?" Charla remarked that her four-year-old twin boys put the twinkle in her eyes. She shared that they light up her life and give her much joy. Charla had been extremely stressed because until recently she was not able to care for them properly or derive pleasure from them. She didn't know what was happening to her and she was frightened. She seemed to be annoyed about every little thing the children would do during the day. She realized that she felt nothing when they cried and this was "the straw that broke the camel's back." Charla could no longer ignore her situation; she knew she needed help and asked her husband to take her to see a psychiatrist who recommended first an inpatient stay of two to three weeks and then outpatient participation in a psychiatric program. The antidepressant Effexor™ and the group therapies seemed to be helping, and Charla was most grateful. She stated that at present she is almost 100 per cent well and hopes to feel cheerful like "her old self" in the near future.

Figure 87

A 32-year-old woman named Megan focused on her accomplishments and "gifts" (family members and friends). She stated that the very shiny stones within the circle represented important people in her life whom she loved very much. The two purple, rectangular stones on the upper left side of the circle symbolize her three-year-old twin girls, and the green heart (center left) represents her husband, Mike. The red center stone symbolizes herself. It is important to note that Megan placed herself in the center of the circle, something she would not have done in the past. She was working on increasing her self-esteem and focusing on herself instead of solely on others. The other, less significant, stones stand for her parents, brother, and best friends. According to Megan, the variety of felt shapes represent achievements such as graduating from college, getting a driver's license and learning how to ski. Megan seemed pleased with her mandala, although she agreed with a peer that it appeared a bit empty. She stated she hoped the empty spaces would fill in as she continued to rediscover her abilities and recover from her depression.

Bottle cap mandala

Materials: An assortment of bottle caps, all sizes and colors. Strong glue or glue gun, and markers.

Procedure: Instruct participants to fill in the mandala with the bottle caps to create a pleasing design, image, or scene. Markers may be used to enhance the design if desired or the mandala may be painted before gluing the bottle caps.

Discussion: Explore organizational and problem solving skills. Examine the creations and their significance. Support group members to reminisce by relating the bottle caps to games they might have played in the past using or substituting pieces for bottle caps (such as skully [12], checkers, or backgammon).

Bead mandala

Materials: Beads of all shapes and sizes, strong glue or glue gun.

Procedure: Group members utilize the beads in any way they please to create an image or design within the circle.

Discussion: Explore colors, patterns, and the organization of the mandala. Observe who put a lot of work into the project and who became easily frustrated. Examine which clients created a balanced work and which clients glued the beads in a haphazard manner. Discuss how various methods of presentation represent characteristics of group participants. Examine ways in which clients identify with various features of their design, such as the shape, size, and placement of certain beads.

Figure 88
Mandala illustrated in the color insert

A woman named Maura, diagnosed with clinical depression, created this attractive bead mandala. Maura took a long time to design this work; she carefully selected each bead and glued them on one by one. She was pleased with the outcome. Maura stated she enjoyed the project because she could work at her own pace and she liked deciding which beads to use. She found it relaxing to glue the beads, making sure they fitted together as closely as possible. Maura related the mandala to various periods in her life. She viewed the mandala as layers of colors and texture. She associated some of the layers to good times she experienced, such as getting married and raising her children. Other layers represented tougher times, such as the death of her husband and losing her home to the bank because she couldn't keep up with the mortgage. The colorful beads symbolized "the fun she has had." Maura viewed some of the larger beads as meaning "not fitting in." She stated that sometimes she feels like she doesn't fit in anymore. She remarked that when she was younger she felt in the center of things, but now that she's 65 she feels "left out of the loop." Maura remarked that it is difficult for her to keep up with the latest technology and language. She wished "the world could be like it used to be." Other group members empathized with her, agreeing that it is not easy to grow old, especially in our society.

Charm necklace mandala

Materials: Drawing paper, markers, crayons, watercolors, water, brushes, colored pencils, and oil pastels.

Procedure: Clients paint within the circle utilizing the color of their choice, preferably a light color. When the paint dries ask participants to draw a chain with charms linked to it (like a charm bracelet). The charms should be large enough so that words or pictures can be placed within them. Next participants fill in the charms with positive and negative thoughts, people, images, ideas, and things in their life. Examples may include a loving relationship, a wonderful family, or problems and depression.

Discussion: Explore the design, size, strength, and length of the chain and charms. Explore the significance of the charms and whether there are many or few of them. Observe whether there are more negative or positive charms and the impact the charms have on one's mood, behavior, and life. Explore the decisions each individual makes each day about choosing to focus on the negative charms (negative aspects of one's life) or positive ones (more positive aspects of life).

Nuts and bolts

Materials: Cardboard, silver paint, markers, glue gun or very strong glue, a variety of small metallic objects such as nuts, bolts, washers, etc.

Procedure: Participants paint the circle silver and let it dry. Next they create a striking mandala by gluing the nuts, bolts, and washers within the circle. Images and shapes may be drawn and/or painted to add to the overall design.

Discussion: Group members share images and associations to the metallic objects that compose the mandala. Encourage participants to relate the nuts, bolts, etc. to thoughts about strength, rehabilitation, and repair. Emphasize that the metallic items are tools used to put things in order. Next ask clients to share their own coping tools and techniques.

Green mandala[13]

Materials: Old CDs, old magazines, bone folder, glass from an broken frame, relief (3D) paint, white craft glue, silicone glue (or hot glue), and beads.

Procedure:

For the magazine coils:

1. Cut a magazine page in two strips. Roll each strip in a diagonal fashion starting from the lower right corner until the upper left corner (you can use a pencil or a barbecue skewer to help and make the rolls).

2. Put a dab of white craft glue on the corner of the strip and press to secure the roll.

3. Make as many rolls as you need for your design.

4. Before making the coils, flatten the rolls first with the bone folder (the back of an Exacto knife or regular knife or the handles of a scissor can also be used). Use the skewer to start forming a coil from this flattened roll. Keep coiling until it reaches the desired size (you can use white craft glue or hot glue to secure the coil as you go).

5. Put a drop of glue on the tip of the roll and press while it dries.

6. Remove the skewer carefully. You can make bigger coils using more than one roll per coil (open the wider tip of the first roll, put a drop of white craft glue, insert the finer tip of the second roll and press while it dries; continue coiling until desired size).

Constructing the mandala:

1. Find the center of your base (glass, acrylic glass, plexiglas, thick cardstock, or other) and mark it (use a water-resistant pen if your base is made of glass or a pencil if you use cardstock).

2. Mark the center of each side of your base.

3. Draw fine lines from the latter marks to the center, to divide your base in eight parts. These lines are only there as guidelines to keep the form symmetrical but will be erased later. (Tip: when using glass you can draw the lines on the back and when the mandala is finished erase them with alcohol.)

4. Clean the CDs with alcohol (shiny side only) and arrange them on your base, using the lines as guides, until you are happy with the design.

5. Glue them in place using silicone glue or hot glue (if the base is cardstock you can use white craft glue). Arrange the magazine coils on the CDs, keeping your design symmetrical. Glue the coils in place with white craft glue or hot glue. Decorate with relief paint pens and beads using your inspiration and creativity. Let dry and erase the lines that are still apparent. (Tip: you can protect your work with a clear sealer like an acrylic varnish spray, or just the coils with diluted craft glue.)

Discussion: Explore thoughts about the completed work and the steps involved. Explore how imagination and resourcefulness may be utilized to create beauty out of "junk." Discuss how it is possible to create meaning and find a purpose even when life seems bleak. This project can be related to the idea of making lemonade from lemons. One can almost always "recycle" their life, "put it together" to create something even more beautiful and meaningful.

Figure 89
Mandala illustrated in the color insert

According to the artist:

> This was the first mandala that I designed and constructed. I was almost mesmerized by the beauty and detail of the traditional Tibetan mandalas, the intricacy of Zen mandalas and all the more western versions. The symmetry, the balance, the beautiful application of colors always seemed fascinating and at the same time unattainable for me. Nevertheless one day I was struggling with inspiration for my work with recycled material and decided to do something different. It started with the old CDs, the magazine rolls (from previous projects) and the old square (therefore symmetric) frame. And last but not least using a color that I seldom use so applying it harmoniously was a challenge. Getting out of the comfort zone is not always easy but can reveal a creative and inspired side of you that you've never known.

Crystals and mandala[14]

Materials: A variety of stones and crystals, water paper, paints, markers, brushes, and water.

Procedure: Select a number of stones and crystals and after taking a few deep breaths and relaxing, move the stones around and form them into patterns. This is a form of active contemplation which can be as valuable as receptive meditation.

It is most traditional to begin in the center point and move from the center outward most often in a clockwise circular direction.

You may want to create the mandala from geometric or traditional spiritual patterns. Many simple crystal mandalas are made in formations identical to the most common crystal grids such as various star, wheel, compass, spiral, and spoke patterns, often with a simple single crystal center. Mandalas, whether in a geometric or intuitive free form with crystals or other media, are most often done in a focused, intentional, dedicated, and meditative or trance state.

Crystal mandala can be made entirely with crystals and stones or crystals and stones might be combined with painted, drawn or sculpted work.

You might select stones in accord with your purpose in creating the mandala, such as those associated with your birth sign and natal chart; dream and archetypal symbolism may also inspire your intuitive mandala.

When making a crystal mandala one generally begins with a focused meditation and places stones either according to a standard pattern or intuitively. I often will take many of my stones and as a meditation place them intuitively in spirals or other patterns as I breathe deeply.

Discussion: While there are many different symbolic traditions that can be used in mandala, one of the most traditional symbol sets, and one considered to have innate power to effect realization, is by using Tattwa (see below). These simple geometric symbols can be used in crystal meditation either by arranging crystals in these forms or by using stones that are shaped like these symbols or by placing stones on key points of a mandala graph comprised of these symbolic forms.

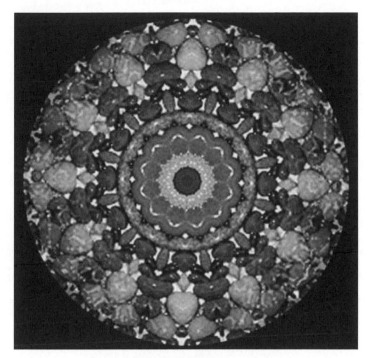

Figure 90
Mandala illustrated in the color insert

Peggy Jentoft: "I had worked with these forms in Tattwa based astrological mandala developed by Michael Matthews of Hayward about a decade ago and they were profoundly transformative."

Tattwa is a Sanskrit word meaning energy. Tattwas are five geometric symbols which represent the five universal energies. Each Tattwa symbolizes unique energies with specific properties, potentials, and frequencies. In varying combinations, these five energies make up the sum totality of everything in our physical and spiritual universe.

These five basic symbols are combined to create symbols of many different kinds. The symbols are the ovoid, the triangle, the half-moon, the circle, and the square. These definitions are minimal and in no way represent the totality of the symbol.

Figure 91

Ovoid or ellipse represents space, the void, the universe, the womb, the cosmic egg, new life, understanding, and female or yin energy.

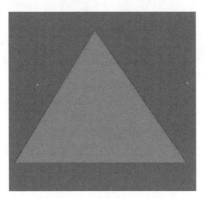

Figure 92

Triangle represents fire and passion. Meditate on this symbol to intensify and clarify desire, creativity, prosperity, and magnetism, and to develop the right brain.

Figure 93

Circle represents air and thought, and is used to enhance ones ability to visualize and discriminate. Meditation on circles activates the subconscious mind and brings about greater ability to discriminate, concentrate and communicate.

Figure 94

Moon represents water; this symbol increases the ability to feel and meditation with this form can bring greater self reflection sensitivity and receptivity toward others.

Figure 95

Squares represent earth, focus, determination, diversity, and inner strength, enhancing the ability to move from dreams to reality.

There are other geometric forms and shapes of crystals that can be used in mandala work. These include the Platonic solids:

- tetrahedron (4 triangular faces): Fire

- hexahedron or cube (6 square faces): Earth

- octahedron (8 triangular faces): Air

- dodecahedron (12 pentagonal faces): Ether and Prana

- icosahedrons (20 triangular faces): Water

- sphere: Void.

Notes

1   www.kinderart.com/painting/tiedye1.shtml, Judith Walsh.

2   Judith Decker is an art educator from Mt. Zion Elementary in Suffolk, VA; *Incredible Art Department*, www.princtonol.com/groups/iad/, accessed 25 October 2012. Also see Kinderart.com. If you have access to a kiln, earthenware clay is preferable. Pieces can be fired to bisque and glazed. Finished pieces can be used as coasters as well.

3   This project is geared for the higher functioning client who is able to focus and follow directions well.

4   "Native American-Mandala", What's Your Sign.com, http://www.whats-your-sign.com/Native-American-mandala.html, accessed July 13, 2012.

5   www.folkartpa.org/Teachers/MandalaWorksheet.pdf, accessed September 27, 2012.

6   The circles may be cut from a light type of wood such as balsa board.

7   Virginia Fleck, http://virginiafleck.com/, accessed July 13, 2012. The instructions are a very simplified version of those of Virginia Fleck. Most client mandalas would be simple designs, unlike Ms. Flecks', which take weeks to months to design and are very beautiful and intricate.

8   National Button Society, www.nationalbuttonsociety.org/Home.html, accessed July 13, 2012.

9   Karen LiCausi www.princetonol.com/groups/iad/files/kara-man.htm The directions have been modified somewhat to suit the needs of clients.

10 Posted on May 12, 2011 by Kathybarbro on http://en.paperblog.com/mandala-drawing-on-an-old-cd–21572/, accessed July 13, 2012.

11 Colored gravel may be purchased at most pet stores where fish and aquariums are sold. The shoelaces may be purchased in various shoe stores and on Amazon.com. Higher functioning clients might want to outline all shapes with the shoelaces for a more dynamic appearance.

12 Skully or Skelly is a children's game, played in New York City by flicking the bottle caps to get them into certain squares, which are drawn with chalk on the ground. See Wikipedia for further details.

13 Mar de Sonho: Handmade crafts by Mar Silva, mardesonho.blogspot.com, accessed July 13, 2012 for more information. This is a detailed and intricate project, and would be presented to high functioning clients in small groups.

14 Peggy Jentoft, Crystals and Mandala, http://pjentoft.com/f-59-crystmandala.html, accessed July 13, 2012. Some examples of digital crystal mandala made from photographs of crystals can be seen at Crystal Mandala Images and more are at Art and mandala.

Chapter 8

Reflective Writing

Incorporating mandala art with creative writing and poetry provides clients with the opportunity to share feelings and experiences in a very personal, safe, and artistic manner. They are in control as they put their thoughts and dreams on paper, sometimes solely within the mandala. The author is in charge of what he writes and how he writes; he can be truthful or fanciful if he wishes. Experiences that are too painful to share verbally can be written and shared only if the author chooses to do so. Creative writing allows the client to reach out to others in a non-threatening manner. It permits him to communicate his feelings and gain a more realistic perspective. After expressing troubling thoughts, the client can view his feelings from a distance and not "own them" so much. He can gain more perspective and analyze his work at his leisure. The writer is given the opportunity to identify, recognize, and process his feelings. Poetry, for instance, become a vehicle for sharing happiness, sadness, fear, frustration, love, and hope. It can lift one's spirits and free the mind. Self-awareness and self-esteem are enhanced. Creating poetry can help clients who are stuck to gain more freedom as they learn to think abstractly.

Poetry can also be used to elicit images that hold significance for clients. Often poems and creative writings bring forth a myriad of feelings, associations, and thoughts, which can be translated into artwork. The mandala provides a safe structure for these personal reflections.

Dancing heart

Materials: Markers, oil pastels, crayons, and drawing paper.

Procedure: Clients read the poem "I Wandered Lonely as a Cloud" and discuss its meaning. Next suggest they represent their "heart dancing" in the mandala. Participants may take this literally and/or portray what makes them feel elated and joyful. They may want to reflect on nature as a way to achieve peace and joy.

Discussion: Explore ways in which the mandalas relate to each participant's personal idea of bliss and to the lovely imagery conveyed in the poem.

I Wandered Lonely as a Cloud

I wandered lonely as a cloud
That floats on high o'er vales and hills,
When all at once I saw a crowd,
A host, of golden daffodils;
Beside the lake, beneath the trees,
Fluttering and dancing in the breeze.

Continuous as the stars that shine
And twinkle on the Milky Way,
They stretched in never-ending line
Along the margin of a bay:
Ten thousand saw I at a glance,
Tossing their heads in sprightly dance.

The waves beside them danced; but they
Out-did the sparkling waves in glee:
A poet could not but be gay,
In such a jocund company:
I gazed—and gazed—but little thought
What wealth the show to me had brought:

For oft, when on my couch I lie
In vacant or in pensive mood,
They flash upon that inward eye
Which is the bliss of solitude;
And then my heart with pleasure fills,
And dances with the daffodils.

William Wordsworth (1804)

Higher power

Materials: Paper plates, drawing paper, pens, pencils, markers, crayons, and oil pastels.

Procedure: Ask participants to outline a circle and write a description or poem in relation to their higher power in it. Suggest that their higher power is personal and could include whomever or whatever they please. Examples are: a religious figure, Buddha, the Dalai Lama, nature art, science, a close friend, family member, their conscience, etc. Next have them design a background reflecting the strength of their faith.

Discussion: Explore how each person's beliefs help him cope. Examine how the client's representation of his higher power affects his attitude and outlook on life.

Written mandala[1]

Materials: Templates of various size circles, drawing paper, crayons, markers and colored pencils.

Procedure: A written mandala is made up of a number of concentric circles, which include positive statements and affirmations. Clients outline a circle and then create at least three to four concentric circles within it. They begin writing from the smallest, innermost circle, working their way outwards in a clockwise direction. All words and sentences are joined in a continuous stream of sentences (no spaces between words). Small pictures and symbols may be interspersed between sentences.

Discussion: Participants share the significance of their writings and explore how the words create a unique design. Clients examine how the process of writing and then reviewing the words is a healing and energizing experience.

Collective mandala

Materials: Mural paper, markers, crayons, oil pastels, and colored pencils.

Procedure: Trace the outline of a large circular object such as the top of a garbage can. Create a number of smaller concentric circles within the large circle. Then have each group member contribute an affirmation or positive sentence to the mandala beginning at the center and working their way outwards, Clients take turns adding a sentence and/or small symbol such as a star or a flower until the mandala is filled up. All words and sentences are joined together.

Discussion: Everyone shares their written contributions and group members explore the overall meaning of the mandala. Group unity, strength, energy, and connectedness are focused upon.

The language of color

Materials: Markers, oil pastels, crayons, colored pencils, and drawing paper.

Procedure: Clients are asked to fill in the mandala with colors and designs. Suggest they think of the colors as a language that will help them to express thoughts and emotions. For instance, red may be fiery and angry; it may say, "I am holding in strong feelings," blue may be calming and it may say, "I am being mindful," and green may be peaceful and comforting, and it may say, "I am feeling safe." After completing the mandala have clients write a poem or description relating to the personal message the colors convey.

Discussion: Explore the significance of the colors of the mandala, and ways in which color affects mood and behavior. Examine the connections between the artwork and the poetry/creative writing, and its meaning for the artist.

Aging

Materials: Drawing paper, markers, oil pastels, crayons, and paper plate.

Procedure: Ask participants to create a mandala that relates to the following poem. Focus on the positive and negative aspects of aging by using pertinent colors, shapes, figures, and symbols.

Aging

Each day is Gold,
As we age.
Nothing is more valuable than time.
I'm mindful; I'm focused,
I'm appreciative too.
But sometimes I wish in the past
I knew,
That time would go by in a blink of the eye,
And life is not always,
A dream come true.
With it comes wisdom and extra free time,
But also comes pain, loss, and resign,
There is good and bad in all of life,
But I still wish I'd stay young all of my life.
I wish I could pick and choose.
I wish I never had much to lose.
But for now I'll just think about today,
Because it's all I have,
Today, today, today.

                    by "L," a female group member

Discussion: Participants share how their mandala relates to the poem and to the theme of aging. Have clients explore encouraging and daunting aspects of getting older.

Word list pass and mandala

Materials: Pencils, pens, drawing paper, markers, oil pastels, crayons, and colored pencils.

Procedure: Ask clients to sign their name at the bottom of their sheet of paper. In this way they know which paper they began working on first. Instruct them to write a positive word or brief phrase on the paper and then ask them to pass their paper to the person sitting to their right (wait a few minutes before asking them to pass their paper so they have time to reflect). Now everyone has a second sheet of paper and they write another positive word on this sheet of paper, and then again they pass the paper to the person on their right.

This keeps happening until everyone has written a positive word on everyone else's paper and the clients receive their original sheet back. They will know it is theirs because they will see their name written on the bottom of the page. Each client should now have a sheet filled with positive words and statements. Next have them outline a circle from a paper plate on a sheet of drawing paper in order to create a mandala. Suggest they create a design within the mandala that reflects feelings associated with the positive words. For example, a mandala that focuses on words like cheerful, friendly, and fun might be filled with colorful shapes, movement, wavy designs or smiling faces, suns, flowers, etc.

Discussion/goals: Discussion focuses on the word lists and the composition of the mandala. Goals include being positive and exploration of attitude, mood and perspectives on life.

This project may need two sessions if there is a time constraint or if clients/leaders feel there are too many steps to follow.

Expressive mandala

Materials: Drawing paper, paper plate, markers, oil pastels, colored pencils, and crayons.

Procedure: On the perimeter of the circle have clients write anything they are presently feeling (mood, energy level, concerns, etc.). Then ask participants to illustrate what they wrote inside the mandala using figures, shapes, colors, lines, and designs.

Discussion: Explore ways in which the words and designs reflect mood, attitude, and behavior.

Mandala inspired poetry

Materials: Drawing paper, markers, pencils, pens, oil pastels, and paper plates.

Procedure: Suggest clients create a mandala of their choice, and then ask them to view it carefully and "listen to what it says to you."

Next have them write a poem or a descriptive paragraph related to the message the mandala conveys.

Discussion: Explore the characteristics of the mandala and its significance. Have clients read their poetry and share how the poems relate to the mandala and to their thoughts, feelings and experiences.

Figure 96
Mandala illustrated in the color insert

A 51-year-old woman challenged with depression created this mandala.

Her associated poem:

My center is a flower,
My family surrounds me.
They are flowers too,
They are purple, pink and green.
Colors of beauty and nature,
I gain energy because of them,
They help me grow,
They love me,
And I love them.

Perseverance

Materials: Drawing paper, paper plates, markers, oil pastels, and crayons.

Procedure: Clients read the following poem, "You Still Have Hope," together and then illustrate what it means to them through the use of color, shapes, figures, and design.

Discussion: Encourage group members to discuss their reaction to the poem and the parts of it that have the greatest significance for them. Explore how the mandalas shed light on the meaning and message of the poem. Have participants share their degree of hopefulness on a 1–10 scale where 10 is the most hopeful and 0 is the least hopeful. Pose the question and explore, "What gives your life meaning, and what gives you the courage to battle your challenges and pursue goals and dreams?"

You Still Have Hope

If you can look at the sunset and smile, then you still have hope.

If you can find beauty in the colors of a small flower, then you still have hope.

If you can find pleasure in the movement of a butterfly, then you still have hope.

If the smile of a child can still warm your heart, then you still have hope.

If you can see the good in other people, then you still have hope.

If the rain breaking on a rooftop can still lull you to sleep, then you still have hope.

If the sight of a rainbow still makes you stop and stare in wonder, then you still have hope.

If the soft fur of a favored pet still feels pleasant under your fingertips, then you still have hope.

If you meet new people with a trace of excitement and optimism, then you still have hope.

If you give people the benefit of the doubt, then you still have hope.

If you still offer your hand in friendship to others that have touched your life, then you still have hope.

If receiving an unexpected card or letter still brings a pleasant surprise, then you still have hope.

If the suffering of others fills you with pain and frustration, then you still have hope.

If you refuse to let a friendship die, or accept that it must end, then you still have hope.

If you look forward to a time or place of quiet and reflection, then you still have hope.

If you still buy the ornaments, put up the Christmas tree or cook the supper, then you still have hope.

If you can look to the past and smile, then you still have hope.

If, when faced with the bad, when told everything is futile, you can still look up and end the conversation with the phrase…"yeah… BUT…" then you still have hope.

Hope is such a marvelous thing. It bends, it twists, it sometimes hides, but rarely does it break. It sustains us when nothing else can. It gives us reason to continue and courage to move ahead, when we tell ourselves we'd rather give in.

Hope puts a smile on our face
When the heart cannot manage.
Hope puts our feet on the path when our eyes cannot see it.
Hope moves us to act
When our souls are confused of the direction.
Hope is a wonderful thing, something to be cherished and nurtured, and something that will refresh us in return.
And it can be found in each of us, and it can bring light into the darkest of places.
Never lose hope!

                                                        author unknown

Self-help

Materials: Drawing paper, markers, paper plate, crayons, and pastels.

Procedure: Have clients read the following poem, "Today I Smiled." Next ask them to fill in the mandala with shapes, colors, figures, and symbols representing positive feelings and methods to take care of oneself physically and psychologically. Encourage group members to use the poem for reference. Examples might include someone exercising, a heart, a flower or bird, a smiling face, etc.

Discussion: Participants share ways in which the mandala reflects specific segments of the poem, its overall message, and self-help measures. Group members examine methods to be more optimistic and ways to gain greater enjoyment out of life.

Today I Smiled

Today I smiled and all at once
Things didn't look so bad.
Today I shared with someone else,
A little bit of hope I had.
Today I sang a little song,
And felt my heart grow light.
I walked a happy little mile,
With not a cloud in sight.
Today I worked with what I had,
And longed for nothing more,
And what had seemed like only weeds,
Were flowers at my door?
Today I loved a little more,
And complained a little less.
And in the giving of myself,
I forgot my weariness.

author unknown

Holding on

Materials: Drawing paper, markers, oil pastels, markers, and crayons.

Procedure: Clients read the following Chinese proverb, interpret it together, and then create a mandala that illustrates the message of the proverb.

> "You cannot prevent the birds of sorrow from flying over your head, but you can prevent them from building nests in your hair."

Discussion: Observe how the mandalas represent themes such as holding grudges, not accepting change, and being stuck. Explore the mandalas that symbolize remaining in the victim role and those that demonstrate freedom and release from obsessing about negative thoughts and issues. View who represented the proverb in a concrete manner and who was able to be more abstract and introspective.

The flag

Materials: Copy of the American flag that is small enough to fit within the mandala, markers, glue, pens, colored pencils, crayons, and scissors.

Procedure: Have clients cut and glue the flag somewhere within the circle. Then suggest they fill in the white stripes with affirmations and statements related to freedom. The rest of the stripes may be colored in with red marker or crayon. A background may be created with images, designs, colors, and shapes.

Discussion: Discussion focuses on the way the flag was designed and placed within the circle. The significance of the phrases written within the mandala may be focused upon. Explore what freedom means for each individual. Examine physical and psychological freedom (e.g. freedom from stress, worries, dependence).

Mandala poetry[2]

Materials: Pens, pencils, markers, crayons, and oil pastels.

Procedure: Clients create an accumulative poem or short story. They brainstorm ideas on a topic, listing a variety of related objects on a whiteboard, e.g. Topic: House; related objects: chair, sofa, bed, lamp, and table. Next each client chooses one of these items and draws a representation of it (realistic or abstract) in the middle of their mandala. Next they write something relating to the characteristics of the object, For example: the chair was slightly worn and faded, but comfortable and cozy. Lastly, one at a time, group members hold up their mandala, share it with peers, and read their narrative. This goes on until everyone has had a chance to share their artwork, and a poem or short story is formed.

Discussion: Explore the significance of the objects chosen and the associated descriptions. Discuss the poem or story formed and group members' reactions to it. Examine how it felt for participants to work together as a team. A sense of community and connecting with others is focused upon.

Notes

1 This project was modified from information found at Mandalas of bright words and gratitude to nature, http://byakkoblog.typepad.com/files/mandala-pamphlet-web.pdf, accessed July 16, 2012. Written mandalas were introduced in Japan in 1999 by Masami Saionji, chairperson of Byakko Shinko Kai, an international organization working for world peace and the elevation of humanity's consciousness.

2 Modified from a project by Jo Hinchliffe Writing workshops, Poetry Session Outline, http://johinchliffe.com/poetry-outline.html, accessed July 16, 2012.

Chapter 9

Kellogg's MARI® Revisited
Archetypal Approach to the Creation and Interpretation of Mandalas
Laura V. Loumeau-May

Mandalas are popular and versatile art therapy tools. Jung prominently advocated the spontaneous emergence of the mandala as a symbol for the Self (1968). Art therapy clinicians typically have clients draw mandalas in a contemplative state, similar to meditation. As demonstrated elsewhere in this book, others use this circular format in innovative, "non-traditional" ways. Following is a discussion of the practices and value of MARI® training. MARI® was developed by Joan Kellogg (2002). It is a systematic analysis of the mandala form that helps the understanding of both the creative process and the resultant product. It illustrates the correspondence of specific archetypal forms or designs that emerge in mandala drawings with the subject's psychological state, including the underlying spiritual processes that guide their creation.

Kellogg pioneered research in the use of mandalas in art therapy. She developed her theory based on recurring design schemas while, "collecting, observing and classifying thousands of patients' mandala drawings" during the 1970s (Cox 2003). To support her research she standardized the materials and instructions offered to clients attending the Maryland Psychiatric Research Center. Each client used a 36 or 48 set of oil pastels and drawing paper with a pre-drawn mandala centered on it. They were instructed to work in an open, meditative manner, allowing images, shapes, or patterns to emerge intuitively. Kellogg noticed characteristics that shaped her theories; the common design patterns and symbols that emerged were correlated with key stages in the clients' psychological, emotional, and spiritual development. Some designs appear more frequently with certain psychiatric diagnoses as well as with other life cycle experiences. Kellogg supported her evolving classifications by comparison with cross-cultural symbolism drawn from mythology, religion, and anthropology. Findings from her research were termed by Kellogg: "The Archetypal Stages of The Great Round of Mandala" (Kellogg 2002).

Kellogg's initial system of assessment consisted of 12 stages, which were developmentally ordered from 1 to 12 around a circle. She later added a stage zero in the center. Each stage was characterized by a visual pattern and function that corresponded to a particular psychological state or conflict. Kellogg defined each stage using metaphoric analogies to Freudian and Eriksonian theories as well as to nature, sexual, and birthing experiences.

Kellogg's 13 stages are:

- Stage #0—Clear Light is graphically characterized by complete emptiness. Situated between stages 12 and 1, it functions as a state of "pre-memory" or "oneness with creation." It represents a passage between the attainment of integration from one cycle before reentering the Great Round on a higher level. Graphically it can be confused with Stage 1. It is best thought of as the "fullness of emptiness" or infinite potential.

- Stage #1—The Void appears as an "empty" yet physical container. It can look like a monochromatic circle, crescent or a spider web. Its functional significance is as the receptacle for something not yet manifested.

- Stage #2—Bliss is filled with repetitive forms. Its function, according to Kellogg is as a "seeding" place where multiple potentialities are contained within, but none has yet taken root.

- Stage #3—The Labyrinth image is a spiral design. Similar to spiral growth prevalent in nature, this form indicates a rapid spiritual or psychological transformational process.

- Stage #4—The Beginning looks like a singular form centered within the circle. This is compared to an embryo and represents the coming into focus of something new.

- Stage #5—The Target pattern is concentric circles. The significance of this stage is either that of constriction or of being pushed out of one's previous existence into a new state of being.

- Stage #6—The Paradoxical Split or Dragon Fight has bilateral or interlocking symmetry, halving the circle. This stage indicates the struggle between internal opposing forces within the Self.

- Stage #7—The Squaring of the Circle is a pattern of quadrants or a square inscribed within the circle. This functions as the resolution of the previous stage and the successful integration of opposite forces.

- Stage #8—The Functioning Ego typically has a star or other multi-sided figure, often with an emphasis on directional movement. This stage is most closely associated with individuality, achievement and mastery of the personal ego.

- Stage #9—Crystallization pattern is intricate, harmonious, complex and many sided. The design is of perfect symmetry. This represents the most stable position of the individual ego in relation to the outer world.

- Stage #10—The Gates of Death has downward movement and/or an "x-ing" out of the mandala. Kellogg describes this as a place of sacrifice where former states of being must end in order to prevent stagnation.

- Stage #11—Fragmentation can be recognized by disintegration of form in a fractured, sometimes pie-like manner. This indicates an internal disintegration from a formerly complete state of self in order for new growth to occur.

- Stage #12—Transcendent Ecstasy features expansion beyond the circumference, combined with a harmonious and luminous use of color. This stage indicates integration of growth or learning into the Self.

Kellogg's theory is a model for transformational growth that is dynamic and flexible. It supports the Jungian concept of individuation as a spiral; it indicates continued growth as different goals are achieved and allows for the shifting of perspectives and meaning as individuals progress through a reflective life. Kellogg has also compared the transitional stages to the inception of an idea through its manifestation in the world and reabsorption into the psyche—now at a new stage of completion (1992). She subdivides the 12 stages that comprise the outer Round into those that mediate between conscious self and the outer world (stages 4 through 10) and those that pertain to unconscious states not in one's immediate awareness (stages 3, 2, 1, 12, and 11 on the lower portion of the Round). She compared the functions of the upper stages to ingesting the external world and the lower stages to both discarding and internalizing (Kellogg 1992). Each quadrant of the Great Round represents a different stage in the life cycle. Another aspect of her conceptualization of the dynamics of the Round was in illustrating the polarities of the stages on various issues such as Power (#5) as opposite to Powerlessness (#11) or Singleness (#8) as opposite to Multiplicity (#2). Kellogg developed theory relating to use of color in mandalas, matching much of her symbolism with the function of color in nature.

In 1980, Joan Kellogg introduced the MARI® card test which she had developed as a tool for assessment and research. By standardizing the archetypal forms that participants were attracted to through their card choices, more accurate assessments could be made. The patterns associated with each stage can take different but related forms. For instance, the spiral can be drawn flat or three dimensionally. Kellogg provided three images for each stage. In administering the test, the selected transparent MARI® cards with images printed on them are placed over 1 of 40 color cards (2 of which are foil) of the same size to refine the stage/color choice. The cards are used in combination with the creation of individual mandalas. When a subject draws a mandala the image may not fit neatly into only one archetypal stage. This presents challenges if the analysis is based on the drawing alone and increases the risk of subjective interpretation. The combination of stages in one mandala may indicate that an individual is experiencing more than one stage or is transitioning between stages. Use of the MARI® cards in combination with the free drawing of a mandala helps clarify the actual stage or stage transition. Administration of the test consists of the selection in order of preference of six MARI®

form and color card combinations with discussion of choices. The initial selection of several card combinations helps specify and refine the stages indicated by the drawing. The choices may reinforce what was drawn or indicate movement away from that stage. Clusters of choices among quadrants, or polarities may be discovered, indicating fixation or conflict. Health and balance may also be demonstrated.

Kellogg's theory of the Great Round of Mandala continues to evolve. Phyllis Frame proposed the addition of a seventh "rejected" card choice (2002). When the "rejected" or least appealing card is chosen, the participant is asked to choose a color background based on their emotional reaction to the card. After this, they are asked to choose an alternative color that would make the rejected card more appealing. Frame added this step in the MARI® assessment in order to explore repressed or denied areas of inquiry. The second "healing" color choice is to help search for a means by which the client might be able to approach the area of difficulty. Expertise in Kellogg's color theory as it relates to each of the stages is necessary to use this effectively.

Cox and Frame, authorities (1995) on the MARI® method, have extended its practices to non-mandala artwork. An example is found in Cox's work with Barry Cohen where the unfocused field of perseverative marks associated with stage 2 (Bliss) were identified in the artwork of clients diagnosed with dissociative identity disorder. In their "Ten Category Model" these researchers labeled this imagery as "Induction" pictures, which represented a protective self-hypnotic process. Cohen and Cox developed the Integrative Method of examining artwork from a synthesis of several theories, including Kellogg's. Cox continues to expand on the theory and has proposed alternate word descriptors for most stages, including Stage #0—Longing, Stage #1—Attaching, Stage #2—Incubating, Stage #6—Confronting, Stage #9—Completing, and Stage #11—Disintegrating.

MARI® research has demonstrated its correlation with a variety of diagnostic categories as well as its effectiveness in outpatient treatment. It is a projective assessment tool in that it correlates specific stage choices with diagnostic indicators. It also incorporates formal element features in its attention to how the space of the circle is handled in certain stages. As an assessment tool it has value in diagnosis and in measurement of treatment progress. As a means for collaborative dialogue to increase insight, it is applicable to work with adult clients in private practice. The test is lengthy to administer, making a complete MARI® assessment impractical for many clinical and institutional settings. Training in the theory does provide valuable assessment skills for the art therapy practitioner that can be applied to both mandala and non-mandala artwork with all clients.

An essential value of the MARI® system is for the individual to invite into consciousness the archetype that is working within, whether the individual is selecting a card that strongly attracts him or her or creating a personal mandala. Stimulating the unconscious through presenting images of the stages influences and enriches the choices that clients make. Often stages are blended in the mandala drawing. Using MARI® cards in conjunction with the creation of mandalas helps clarify the movement between stages. This tool activates, bringing particular configurations into conscious awareness and focus. Using the MARI® system as an asset in assessment helps the clinician in treatment planning and in suggesting areas of inquiry with the client. Direct interpretation to the client should be avoided. Instead, the client should be empowered to find her or his own meaning through contemplation of the mandalas created and dialogue around the functioning of the emergent imagery.

Figure 97

Collage mandala, intended to be a spider web (Stage 1), is actually Stage 11 (Fragmentation).

Figure 98

This mandala has characteristics of Stage 4 (Beginning), Stage 3 (Labyrinth), Stage 7 (Squaring of the Circle), and Stage 12 (Transcendent Ecstasy). It was created by Laura Salley ATR–BC.

References

Barreda, P.P. (2008) *Mandala: Spiritual Visions of Our Ancient Self.* Charleston, SC: BookSurge Publishing.

Buchalter, S. (2004) *A Practical Art Therapy.* London: Jessica Kingsley Publishers.

Buchalter, S. (2009) *Art Therapy Techniques and Applications.* London: Jessica Kingsley Publishers.

Buchalter, S. (2011) *Art Therapy and Creative Coping Techniques for Older Adults.* London: Jessica Kingsley Publishers.

Cohen, B.M. and Cox, C.T. (1995) *Telling without Talking: Art as a Window into the World of Multiple Personality Disorder.* New York: W. W. Norton.

Cohen, B.M. and Cox, C.T. (2002) *Exploring the Common Ground between Personality and Artmaking.* Presentation paper, American Art Therapy Association Conference, Washington, D.C.

Cox, C.T. and Cohen, B.M. (2000) 'Mandala artwork by clients with DID: Clinical observations based on two theoretical models.' *Art Therapy Journal of the American Art Therapy Association 17,* 3, 195–201.

Cox, C.T. (2003) 'The MARI Assessment.' In C. Malchiodi (ed.) *Handbook of Art Therapy.* New York: Guilford Press.

Cox, C.T. (2010) *Cycles of the Self; Finding Meaning in Mandalas.* Conference paper, Expressive Therapies, Summit, NYC.

Cox, C.T. and Frame, P. (2007) *The Art of Connecting with Theory: Viewing Artwork through a New Lens.* Presentation paper, American Art Therapy Association Conference, Albuquerque, NM.

Dellios, R. (2003) *Mandala: From sacred origins to sovereign affairs in traditional Southeast Asia.* Research report. Bond University: School of Humanities and Social Sciences: Centre for East-West Cultural and Economic Studies.

Fontana, D. (2009) *Meditating with Mandalas.* New York: Metro Books.

Frame, P. (2002) 'The value of the rejected card choice in the MARI® card test.' *Art Therapy Journal of the American Art Therapy Association 19,* 1, 28–31.

Frame, P. (2006) 'Assessing a couple's relationship and compatibility using the MARI® card test and mandala drawings.' *Art Therapy Journal of the American Art Therapy Association 23,* 1, 23–29.

Jung, C. G. (1968) *Man and His Symbols.* New York: Dell Publishing.

Jung, C. G. (1972) *Mandala Symbolism.* Princeton, NJ: Princeton University Press.

Jung, C. G., (1973) *Mandala Symbolism.* (A collection of three works translated by R. F. C. Hull.) Princeton, NJ: Princeton University Press.

Jung, C.G. and Jaffé, A. (1962) *Memories, Dreams, Reflections.* London: Collins.

Jung, C.G. and Jaffé, A. (1965) *Memories, Dreams, Reflections.* New York: Random House.

Jung, C.G. and Jaffée, M. (1989) *Memories, Dreams and Reflections.* New York: Random House

Kellogg, J. (1992) 'Color therapy from the perspective of the Great Round of Mandala.' *Journal of Religion and Psychic Research 15,* 3, 138–146.

Kellogg, J. (2002) *Mandala: Path of Beauty.* Bellair, FL: Association for Teachers of Mandala Assessment.

Index of Projects

Index